# INDEPENDENT SECTOR

INDEPENDENT SECTOR is a coalition of 830 corporations, foundations, and voluntary organizations with national interests in
and impact on philanthropy, voluntary action, and other
activities related to the educational, scientific, cultural, and
religious life, as well as the health and welfare, of the nation.

INDEPENDENT SECTOR is a meeting ground where diverse elements
in and related to the sector can come together and learn how
to improve their performance and effectiveness.

INDEPENDENT SECTOR is serving the sector through
- education, to improve the public's understanding of the independent sector
- research, to develop a comprehensive store of knowledge about
  the sector
- government relations, to coordinate the multitude of intercon-
  nections between the sector and the various levels of government
- encouragement of effective sector leadership and management,
  to maximize service to individuals and society, by promoting
  educational programs for managers and practitioners
- communication within the sector, to identify shared problems
  and opportunities

The impact of INDEPENDENT SECTOR's effort can be measured by the
growth in support of the sector, as manifested by increased
giving and volunteering.

For additional information, please contact

INDEPENDENT
SECTOR

1828 L Street, N.W.
Washington, DC 20036
(202) 223-8100

# THE
# NONPROFIT
# LOBBYING
# GUIDE

# Bob Smucker

# THE NONPROFIT LOBBYING GUIDE

*Advocating Your Cause—
and Getting Results*

 Jossey-Bass Publishers

San Francisco  •  Oxford  •  1991

THE NONPROFIT LOBBYING GUIDE
*Advocating Your Cause—and Getting Results*
by Bob Smucker

Copyright © 1991 by: Jossey-Bass Inc., Publishers
350 Sansome Street
San Francisco, California 94104

&

Jossey-Bass Limited
Headington Hill Hall
Oxford OX3 0BW

**Library of Congress Cataloging-in-Publication Data**

Smucker, Bob, date.
  The nonprofit lobbying guide: advocating your cause—and getting
results / Bob Smucker.
      p.    cm.—(The Jossey-Bass nonprofit sector series)
  Includes bibliographical references and index.
  ISBN 1-55542-374-4
  1. Lobbying—United States—Handbooks, manuals, etc.
  2. Lobbying—Law and legislation—United States—Handbooks,
manuals, etc.   I. Title.   II. Series.
JK1118.S68    1991
324′.4′0973—dc 20                                          91-2703
                                                            CIP

Manufactured in the United States of America

The paper in this book meets the guidelines for
permanence and durability of the Committee on
Production Guidelines for Book Longevity of the
Council on Library Resources.

JACKET DESIGN BY WILLI BAUM

FIRST EDITION

*Code 9169*

INDEPENDENT
SECTOR    A publication of INDEPENDENT SECTOR

*The Jossey-Bass*
*Nonprofit Sector Series*

*To a good friend and colleague,*
*Skip Helsing*

# CONTENTS

ix

# PREFACE

This is a handbook for volunteers and staff of nonprofit organizations, especially new volunteers and staff, to help them take advantage of the new and exceedingly liberal rules for lobbying by nonprofits.\* These rules now make it possible for nonprofit groups to lobby more freely for their causes and clients. It is very clear that the federal government, including Congress and the Internal Revenue Service (IRS), supports lobbying by nonprofits. Congress sent that unambiguous message when it enacted the generous provisions in the 1976 lobby law.\*\* The same message came from the IRS, in new regulations issued on August 31, 1990, which support both the spirit and the intent of the 1976 legislation. Together, the law and the new regulations provide much more leeway for lobbying than most nonprofits will ever need—or want.

It is my hope that this book will encourage volunteers and staff of nonprofits to be bold in their lobbying to enact laws and pass appropriations that will aid those they seek to serve. I intend

---

\**Nonprofit organization,* as used throughout this book, refers only to organizations that are tax-exempt under Section 501(c)(3) of the Internal Revenue Code.

\*\*The term *1976 lobby law* is used throughout this book for legislation passed in 1976—Section 1307 of PL 94-455—that clarifies and expands lobbying by tax-exempt nonprofits under Section 501(c)(3) of the Internal Revenue Code. The legislation does not apply to churches, their integrated auxiliaries, or conventions or associations of churches.

the book especially for volunteers and staff who are concerned about helping to achieve greater equity in the sharing of this nation's vast resources—people who are working to change public policy in order to assist the most vulnerable in our society.

Those who are new to nonprofit volunteer or staff work may be inclined to place lobbying at the bottom of the list of abilities they want to develop. They may believe that it is too complex to master, perhaps a bit tainted, and maybe even illegal, or they may assign it low priority because they already have a number of other well-honed skills that they can immediately put to work for their organizations. Once involved in the process, however, most people find that lobbying is not difficult to learn, and that the organizing skills they already possess are easily transferred to influencing legislation for the people they serve. And, far from its being disreputable or illegal, most people discover that lobbying is a perfectly legitimate, reasonable, and personally rewarding way of fulfilling their organizations' public purposes.

If you are just getting started, the lobbying tips offered in this book should be helpful as you make your first contacts with legislators. But even if you are not altogether new to lobbying and are looking for additional ideas for your work, you will find a full menu. If you are more experienced at lobbying but are, for example, at the crucial point where you seek a sponsor for legislation that your group wants introduced, I think you will find the strategic advice in this book helpful.

## Organization of the Book

*The Nonprofit Lobbying Guide* is divided into two parts. Part One provides how-to information on lobbying by charities. Almost every national organization has written a manual on how to influence legislation. Each nonprofit's organizational structure is different, and so it is not possible to provide detailed how-to information that will fit every group's needs. There are, however, some approaches to lobbying that seem to accomplish the job for almost all nonprofits, and those approaches are included here.

Part Two gives information, in laypersons' language, concerning a number of technical questions: How much lobbying by nonprofits is legal under federal law? How do the new IRS regulations on lobbying by nonprofits affect the amount of lobbying you can do? Can a private foundation grant funds to a nonprofit that lobbies? What information on the views of a candidate for public office can a nonprofit provide to its members? Should an individual who lobbies for a nonprofit register with federal or state government?

Most of the technical information applies equally to lobbying at the federal, state, and local levels. Part One, the "how-to" section, however, deals principally with federal legislation, although much of the information is readily adapted to state or local lobbying.

In all candor, parts of this book may be less than compelling and will not tempt you to burn the midnight oil. Therefore, I have included a summary in Resource A for readers interested in skimming the book quickly for the main points.

The other resources contain material helpful to lobbyists. Resource B offers answers to some often-asked questions about lobbying; Resource C reprints the article "How to Win the Advocacy Game," by Doug Siglin; Resource D consists of examples of lobbying materials to help you get started; Resource E reprints IRS form 5768, which a nonprofit must file to elect to come under the provisions of the 1976 lobby law; and Resource F lists addresses of organizations that are mentioned in the book so that you can contact them for additional information.

This book, especially Part Two, is intended to provide enough information so that new volunteers and staff will have an elementary understanding of lobbying and will know where to find more information. It is not intended to replace legal counsel. If you have questions regarding the technical information, you should seek legal advice. However, it is important to keep in mind that lawyers, with some notable exceptions, tend to be much too cautious in counseling nonprofits about lobbying. Their usual advice is to tread very lightly, if at all, in the lobbying arena. That's questionable advice, at best, stemming from the fact that too many lawyers are not well acquainted with the lobbying law. It is perfectly acceptable to probe the advice of lawyers, so that you can be very certain that they know the latitude permitted to nonprofits under the law, including the 1976 lobby law.

The Nonprofit Lobbying Guide grew out of what I have learned over the past twenty-five years from lobbying on behalf of nonprofit organizations and working with some extraordinarily talented volunteer and staff lobbyists. I hope it will be a useful guide, but it is simply that: a guide. You don't need to know or practice most of what is in this book to get started lobbying. Don't be put off by what may appear to be a mountain of information. Skim through it, take what you need—and good luck!

## Acknowledgments

Virtually all the information in Chapter Nine was drawn from materials prepared for INDEPENDENT SECTOR by Walter B. Slocombe of Caplin and Drysdale, Washington, D.C. I am grateful that INDEPENDENT SECTOR and Mr. Slocombe have permitted me to use that important information.

Substantial portions of Chapter Ten were taken, with permission, from writings of Sandford F. Brandt. As a volunteer for both the National Mental Health Association and INDEPENDENT SECTOR, Brandt has written on many issues related to lobbying. I am grateful that he permitted me to excerpt so fully from his writings. I am also grateful for his very helpful suggestions on this book.

Final decisions regarding the content of this book were mine, but I owe much to others for their critiques and suggestions. They include Mathew Ahmann, Gary Bass, Philip Berstein, Gregory L. Colvin, John Colvin, Lee Goodman, Julee Kryder-Coe, Brian O'Connell, Hilda Robbins, Walter B. Slocombe, Barbara Mills Smucker, Thomas A. Troyer, and Edward T. Weaver. I am especially indebted to Brenda Lee, who typed and edited numerous revisions of the manuscript.

Washington, D.C.                                          Bob Smucker
June 1991

# THE AUTHOR

Bob Smucker, vice-president for government relations at INDEPEN-DENT SECTOR since 1980, has worked with nonprofit organizations since 1957. His background includes twenty-five years as a lobbyist at the local, state, and national levels.

From 1957 to 1971, he worked in Pennsylvania with local mental health associations, as well as with the Pennsylvania Mental Health Association, a statewide citizens' advocacy organization. During that time, his lobbying activities included a leading role in the enactment of legislation, passed in 1966, that provided for the development and funding of community mental health centers. He was also involved in a successful effort to get the United Steel Workers of America to include ambulatory mental health coverage in its nationwide contract with the steel industry.

From 1971 to 1979, Smucker was director of public policy for the National Mental Health Association. During that time, he was centrally involved in the enactment of the 1976 lobby law, which clarified and expanded the lobbying rights of nonprofits. He was also a principal actor in obtaining continued federal funding for community mental health centers. He had chief responsibility for developing a mental health coalition that brought successful litigation resulting in the release of $127 million in impounded mental health research and training funds by the Department of Health, Education and Welfare. He also provided staff leadership for litigation brought by the National Mental Health Association and other groups in the successful effort to end unpaid patient labor in state mental hospitals.

The author's activities with INDEPENDENT SECTOR have included working with the advocacy community to organize and provide leadership for the coalition that convinced the Internal Revenue Service to withdraw restrictive proposed regulations governing lobbying. That coalition also worked with the IRS to develop sound new regulations. The author also had senior staff responsibility in developing and providing coordination for a coalition that acted to have the Office of Management and Budget withdraw proposed regulations that would have greatly curtailed the rights of nonprofits to lobby with the funds they receive from private contributions. Smucker has also had principal staff responsibility for INDEPENDENT SECTOR's involvement in three Supreme Court cases related to the fund-raising activities of nonprofits. All three cases were decided in favor of the First Amendment rights of nonprofits.

# THE
# NONPROFIT
# LOBBYING
# GUIDE

# Part One

# HOW TO LOBBY

# 1

# Anyone
# Can Lobby

The personnel manager of a large midwestern manufacturing company once told me that job descriptions, even for junior executives, are often drawn up by well-intentioned but unknowing staff to include requirements so demanding that not even the president of the company could fulfill them. How-to books can suffer from the same problem. They don't distinguish between what you have to know and all the other things that could be helpful but are not absolutely essential.

The information in this book is not a description of what you need to know—or the experience you must have—to get started. Nobody, not even the most seasoned lobbyist, does all or even close to half of it. All your organization needs as you start lobbying is a staff person or volunteer who has a little knowledge of lobbying techniques; has an elementary understanding of how the legislative process works in whatever body you are planning to lobby, whether Congress, the state legislature, county government, or the city council; can organize a government relations committee that will consider the legislative issues your organization may want to tackle; can organize volunteers to form a legislative network; and has a passing knowledge of the law governing lobbying by nonprofits.

Much of the information you need to start lobbying probably is readily available in your own community. A number of nonprofits, civic organizations, and public-spirited citizens have been lobbying for years and would be complimented if your group asked them for help in understanding the areas just described. For example, the League of Women Voters could be particularly helpful. Several other groups, including environmental organizations and most of the major health groups (such as the Heart, Lung, Cancer, Mental Health, and Mental Retardation Associations), would have considerable lobbying knowledge and would probably have affiliates in your community.

## Lobbying Law

Before you start lobbying, you should know a little about the law governing lobbying by nonprofits. The 1976 lobby law and regulations provide very generous lobbying limits. You should know what the law says about how much of your organization's annual expenditures can go for lobbying and what activities are defined as lobbying, but the most important point to keep in mind is that the law permits ample room for all the lobbying your group will probably want to undertake. It is very simple to elect to come under the provisions of the law (see Chapter Nine for details).

If you have questions about whether the amount of lobbying you want to conduct is within the law, discuss it with other nonprofits that lobby extensively, as well as with your attorney. But remember that attorneys almost always err on the side of extreme caution in counseling nonprofits about lobbying. If you ask your lawyer for advice, be certain that he or she not only knows the lobby law well (only a few do) but, even more important, also is familiar with the experience of organizations that have lobbied under the law. Groups have found plenty of legal latitude for lobbying, without jeopardizing their tax-exempt status.

## The Legislative Process and Your Lobbyist

It is important to have a volunteer or staff person in your organization who knows the basics of how your legislature works, because you will need that information to know how to target your efforts. For example, you may be trying to block legislation averse to your group, help support pending legislation backed by your organization, or arrange the introduction of legislation vital to your group. In the typical legislature, to achieve any of these aims, you will have to gain the support of the committee designated to consider your issue. It follows that you will need to know something about the composition of that committee. For example, if you are seeking to have legislation introduced, it is usually possible to recruit a committee member to introduce your bill. But you won't want just any member. You will want a person of influence, and that usually means a senior committee member whose party is in the majority and therefore controls the committee.

It is incidentally helpful to know that many decisions on legislation are often made in a last-minute frenzy as legislators prepare to adjourn for the legislative session. The lobbyist (whether a volunteer or a paid staff member) who is following your issue in the legislature should have enough understanding of how the legislative process works so that your group can make the right move at the right place and time (for example, knowing whether to support or oppose an amendment that suddenly comes up). Your lobbyist needs to recognize, for example, whether this is the last chance to modify your bill or if you still have a reasonable chance for the changes you want in the other house of the legislature. A lobbyist who knows (among other things) the best legislator to introduce your bill and how and when decisions are made in your legislature is referred to as an *inside lobbyist*.

Having a seasoned insider available to your organization can save you enormous time and effort. Perhaps volunteers or staff people bring such experience to your group from their work with other nonprofits. If not, such groups as the League of Women Voters can help your group develop an understanding of how your legislature really works. Former legislators or those currently in office can also be very helpful. Nationally, the Advocacy Institute and INDEPENDENT SECTOR, among other organizations, can provide how-to information about lobbying by nonprofits (see Resource F).

If you have the funds, it is possible to hire a good, experienced lobbying consultant. If you choose that route, check with other nonprofits whose opinions you value highly and who have used consultants to lobby. The best way of being certain that you are getting the right person is to check his or her track record with other groups. Consultants should be pleased to give you the names of groups for which they have lobbied.

### The Government Relations Committee
### and the Legislative Network

Your organization will need to set up a government relations committee to consider how your group's program can be furthered by legislative initiatives. The committee will also establish legislative priorities and provide direction for the group's lobbying efforts. A strong government relations committee that represents a broad cross-section of your community can add immeasurably to the impact of your lobbying efforts. In using a government relations committee, it is enormously important to hold firmly to one top legislative priority, rather than following the more common route of trying to work on many issues at once. (This point and others are covered in Chapter Seven.)

A nonprofit's principal lobbying power resides in the number of its members that it can get behind its legislation. To achieve that objective, most groups set up a legislative network to mobilize the grass-roots network (see Chapter Four). At the minimum, your network should assign *one* volunteer, capable of enlisting others in his or her community, as a contact person for *each* member of the legislative committee(s) that will act on your bill. If there are twenty members of a legislative committee that will act on your bill, twenty contact persons should be recruited.

Establishing and maintaining the network takes time and commitment because it is tedious, time-consuming work. It is easy to put off establishing a network and even easier to neglect it once it is set up. A nonprofit neglects its network at great risk, however. Without a network, there may be no chance to mobilize broad support on short notice. That kind of quick mobilization may be needed repeatedly during a legislative campaign.

In short, you need very little to get started. As we have seen, it helps to have a volunteer or a staff person who has an elementary understanding of basic lobbying techniques and of the lobbying process, as well as some organizing skills. As in all activities that involve people, common sense helps immeasurably.

Don't be put off by the amount of information in this book. If you can pick up a pen or the phone, you can lobby. Just go ahead. Get started, and keep in mind that lobbying and the legislative process are not nearly as complicated or difficult as lobbyists would have you believe.

# 2

# The
# Nonprofit Lobbyist
# and the
# Legislative Process

A nonprofit's power to affect legislation comes from its grass-roots strength—the quality and number of letters, other communications, and personal contacts its members make with legislators. Every one of an organization's members who communicates with a legislator is, in a very real sense, a lobbyist. Nevertheless, every organization that participates in the legislative process needs a volunteer or staff lobbyist who has some in-depth knowledge of the legislative process and can help provide direction for the group's legislative activities. This chapter describes the work of that principal lobbyist. A nonprofit's principal power does not reside in its lobbyist at the capital, because he or she does not live, work, and vote in the legislator's district. But a skilled lobbyist, whether a volunteer or a paid staff member, can contribute greatly to the development of the group's impact on legislation by providing effective liaison between the legislature and the nonprofit's grass roots.

Many nonprofits that are just starting to lobby recruit volunteers who have knowledge of and some experience with the legislative process. Over time, such groups often hire part-time or full-time staff or consultants to augment their lobbying capability. Many others continue very effectively with volunteers in the principal lobbying role. The important point is that you don't need a paid lobbyist to get started or even to conduct a sophisticated lobbying program. The League of Women Voters, for example, has few paid lobbyists, but the group is well known and respected for the skills its volunteers bring to government relations, including lobbying.

To get started, your lobbyist needs to know or be able to learn quickly the following things:

- The basics about the legislative process and the key committee members or other legislators who have either jurisdiction or influence over your legislation and can affect its movement
- The details of the bill you are supporting and why its provisions are important to the legislators' constituents and to your organization
- The organizational structure of your group and how it communicates with its grass roots.

More important, the person who will be your lobbyist should have strong skills in interpersonal relations. A prospective lobbyist for your group may bring great understanding of government, its processes and its key members, but if the relationship skills are absent, don't give him or her the job. This candidate will lack the most fundamental attribute of a good nonprofit lobbyist. It would be better to take on a person who has no lobbying experience but has demonstrated interpersonal skills and the ability to organize. Most such persons can be taught to lobby, but chances are that you will not be able to change the performance of the person who brings understanding of the process but lacks sound interpersonal skills.

You will be tempted to take the person who lacks the relationship skills but has the knowledge, especially if he or she is articulate. If you do, however, over time you will probably find yourself following after the lobbyist at the state capitol and trying to mend relationships. Worse yet, word won't get back to you about your lobbyist because of people's natural reluctance to pass along negative information; you will just find that your lobbyist is having difficulty gaining access. Again, if you have to make the choice, go with the relationship and organizing skills.

The principal responsibility of your nonprofit group's lobbyist is to work effectively for enactment of your group's legislation. The success or failure of your legislation depends considerably on how well your lobbyist can orchestrate the movement of your bill through the legislature and on how effective he or she is in mobilizing your grass roots. Both tasks require an understanding of the legislative process. More important, the movement of your legislation requires that you recruit a strong member of the legislature to take the lead on your measure.

## The Legislative Process

You are interested in the legislative process because of something you want—or do not want—legislators to do. To be most effective in influencing the legislative process, you must have a feel for how it works.

Legislation begins with the executive (the president, the governor, and so on), or it starts with an individual member of the legislature. Once started, the legislation goes to committees of both houses, and then it is acted on by one house, after which it goes to the other house and finally to a conference committee. The conference committee, composed of members of both houses, works out any differences between versions of the legislation passed by the two houses. The measure ultimately goes to the executive, to be either signed into law or vetoed. At each step, the measure can be stopped, changed, or passed along to the next stage of the process. Those decisions are made by individual members of the committee to which the legislation is referred, or they are made by the full House or Senate if the measure has moved out of committee. Each step can be influenced by your organization, as can the executive's decision to sign or veto the bill.

## The Nonprofit's Legislative Proposal

Legislation initiated by a nonprofit group usually starts with a program idea that the group thinks would not only make good public policy but also help achieve its own mission. Typically, such a proposal is considered first by the nonprofit's government relations committee and then by its board. Next, according to the importance of the proposed legislative initiative, the proposal may go before the organization's total membership. Early in this process, it will be important for the organization to get information about the viability of the legislative proposal from a person who knows both the legislature and the major forces that will be working for or against the measure.

## Selecting Your Leader in the Legislature

The key step in the legislative process is moving your bill to a successful vote in committee. Virtually no major legislation is enacted without having been considered by committee. Once that hurdle is passed, prospects are usually good for the bill's enactment by that house. Central to your success is the strength of the committee member who has agreed to take the lead on your measure. A skilled lobbyist, whether a volunteer or a staff member, can be enormously helpful to you in recruiting the right person. You will want to choose the most influential committee member of the party that controls the committee. Likewise, for bipartisan balance, you will also want to approach the strongest person from the minority side of the committee to join in leading the effort. Often, of course, you won't be able to enlist the most influential committee members; they will be very much in demand among many other groups. You may have to adjust your sights and turn to another consideration: commitment to your issue, another important criterion in selecting your leader. Recruiting a committee member who is influential but does not strongly support your measure can easily lead to disappointment and probably defeat, especially if your bill is competing in committee with other bills that the legislator supports more strongly.

A criterion of almost equal importance is the skill and commitment of the legislative staff person whom your legislative leader assigns to your measure. A strong, skilled staff person who likes your issue can sometimes compensate for his or her boss's modest interest and power within the committee. Conversely, lack of skill and interest on the part of this staff member can add significantly to the difficulty of moving your measure through, even if the legislator has influence with the committee and likes your issue. On balance, a skilled staff person working for a legislator who has more than a passing interest in your bill is a strong combination. Knowledge about the influence and power of the actors, both legislators and staff, is what your lobbyist must bring to your organization.

## Introducing Legislation

To have legislation drafted, a member of Congress may consult with the legislative counsel of the House or Senate to frame the ideas in suitable legislative language and form. In Congress, the legislation is introduced on the floor of the House and the Senate, and it is assigned a bill number. Members who introduce legislation are called sponsors, and they often submit statements to the *Congressional Record* providing the rationale for their support. A *Congressional Record* statement may be an important resource for a nonprofit in generating support for a measure. Often, the member of Congress also issues a press release or similar statement about the legislation, which describes the measure's importance in language that is easy for a nonprofit to adapt for use with its members.

After the legislation is introduced, the Rules Committee in each house assigns it to the committee responsible for considering its type of legislation. The nonprofit should seek bipartisan support for its proposal by recruiting strong backing from Democrats and Republicans on the committees to which the legislation is assigned. (The nonprofit's members will also be most likely to give their own strong support if both parties are well represented.)

Soon afterward, the sponsors may send a letter, called a "Dear Colleague" letter, to every member of their house or to every member of their committee, explaining why they have introduced the measure and inviting members of their house to sign on as cosponsors. Because the number of members who cosponsor a bill gives an indication of support for the measure, nonprofits, working through local affiliates, often strive hard to recruit a large number of cosponsors. The number of cosponsors is not the true test of a bill's strength, however. Its strength is tested in the committee to which it is referred.

### Role of the Committee

After the bill is assigned to a committee, the chair of the committee sends it to the appropriate subcommittee for consideration. Favorable action on the measure at the subcommittee and full committee levels is almost always a "make or break" situation for the measure. If it succeeds in getting out of subcommittee (especially with a strong majority of members voting in support), it *usually* gets favorable consideration in the full committee. Full committees do not like to second-guess the work of their subcommittees, and so they are often inclined to accept in its entirety, or only with modest modifications, the legislation coming out of their subcommittees.

It is crucial that each member of the subcommittee be contacted by a number of constituents who support the legislation. That is the most important action that a nonprofit can take. If you can't get favorable action in subcommittee, your proposal will have little chance of becoming law. The next most important step is to contact all members of the full committee and enlist their support. A bill may be lodged in committee for a year or longer, so there is usually ample time for a nonprofit to generate continuing grassroots contact with committee members.

Subcommittees and full committees often hold hearings on legislation, to get the views of a diverse group of individuals, organizations, and businesses supporting or opposing a measure. Nonprofits are wise to work closely with committees in setting up hearings and ensuring that there will be witnesses who favor their positions (see Chapter 5). Hearings can be very important in building support for your proposal. Nevertheless, they pale by comparison with the importance of being certain that each committee member is contacted by a number of key constituents who support the legislation.

After hearings, a subcommittee meets to do its final decision making (called a *mark-up*) on the bill and votes on it. By the time the mark-up stage arrives, most members of the committee will have decided whether they support the measure, and so nonprofits dare not wait until that point to make their contacts. That work has to be done in the previous weeks, months, and even years.

Representatives of the nonprofit will want to be present when the legislation is marked up. (Congressional mark-ups are often closed, and so you'll have to wait in the hall outside the conference room. Be assured that you will have plenty of company.) The sponsor of the legislation may find that the only way your proposal can receive a favorable vote is through compromise. The legislator or the legislator's staff person must be able, on a moment's notice, to contact a spokesperson for the nonprofit and find out whether the compromise is acceptable. Before the mark-up, the person speaking for the nonprofit has to have been given authority to negotiate a compromise.

There are several other important reasons for being present at a mark-up. Some committee members may still be undecided, and getting a last-minute word with them can be important. (But, again, don't rely on last-minute contacts; seldom will they win the day.) Another reason for being there is that, by your presence, you are sending a message to legislators that your organization is very interested in the outcome and will be reporting the committee's action to the members' constituents.

### Action on the House and Senate Floors

If your bill fails to make it out of the House committee, it will be virtually impossible to get it considered by the full House. Because the House Rules Committee rarely permits a vote unless a measure has received favorable committee action, the committee vote in the House usually seals the fate of your measure.

In the Senate, leadership may agree to allow a bill to be considered by the full Senate, even if the bill has lost in committee, especially if the committee vote was close. When the Senate sponsor of your legislation is successful in persuading leadership to bring your bill up for a vote in the full Senate, it may be possible for you to win, if you have broad grass-roots support. That can happen only if, in the months and even years before, you have been carefully building support for the measure among all members of the Senate.

### The House/Senate Conference

After legislation has been passed by the House and the Senate, it goes to conference. Conferees are named by the chairs of the committees that have considered legislation. They are usually committee members with the most seniority or are chairs of particular subcommittees. Because conferees are often named a week or so before a conference, it is possible to get some last-minute messages in from the grass roots, if you are following the process closely. You will need to get the list of conferees immediately and get the word out right away, letting your members know what the deadline is for getting their messages to the conferees before the vote. For the same reasons that your group should be represented at a committee mark-up, it is very important to be present at the mark-up by conferees.

### *Action by the President*

The president either signs a bill into law or vetoes it. If the president vetoes the bill, the veto can be overturned only by a two-thirds vote in both houses.

Your organization will usually know well in advance whether the president supports your legislation. If a veto is a possibility, your grass roots will have to be mobilized immediately after Congress passes the legislation, because the president is required to take action on a bill ten days (not counting Sundays) after it is received from Congress. It takes strong grass-roots support to enact legislation, and that support can be enormously influential in persuading an undecided president to sign.

If a bill is vetoed, both houses usually take action to override the veto within a few days. It will be important for you to know of a presidential veto within hours, if not minutes. Once again, your grass-roots supporters should be contacted immediately and urged to get in touch with their senators and representatives, in support of a veto override. Often there will not be time for you to get an alert out to the field and letters back in from the grass roots, so you must be prepared to telephone your grass-roots supporters and have them phone their positions to members of Congress or take other action that is equally speedy.

### Facts About Legislators and the Legislative Process

It is important to remember that all members of a legislature are not equal. For example, majority party members may be more helpful to you than minority members. Majority party members control the particular house of Congress, and its members are chairs of the committees. The chairs have considerable power over committees' decisions. Moreover, senior members may also be more helpful, since they often have significant influence over committees' decisions, and they are more likely to be appointed to conference committees, where key decisions are made. Finally, some members of a committee may be more active than others, for a variety of reasons, including the impact that a committee's legislative agenda may have on legislators' home districts.

While it is important to understand the legislative process, the fact that it is a process run by people makes it also important to put yourself in legislators' shoes. (For an exceptionally lively description of the people, pulls, and pressures in Congress, see Resource C, by Doug Siglin.) Try to understand how you would respond if you were in their position and were being contacted by your organization. Remember that legislators have many votes on their minds and demands on their time. They cannot learn about each issue in the same depth as you know your issues. It is important to be patient with the legislator who does not seem to understand the program you are backing. If the legislator cannot help you on your issue this time, give him or her the benefit of the doubt. Don't take it personally. Maybe the legislator will be with you next time.

The federal government and many state governments provide detailed information on the legislative process. Willett (1990) provides very useful information about the legislative process in Congress, taking a bill step by step from introduction through enactment. It is important for the beginning lobbyist to know the basics of the process, so that he or she will know which questions to ask. Books on the legislative process can help, but it is often even more helpful to get information from people in the legislature. They can help you understand how the process works in practice, and they will probably feel complimented that you have come to them for direction. For example, it is crucial to know that few steps in the process are likely to be critical to the fate of your legislation. The person who will help you the most in knowing which steps are most important is almost always the legislator who has taken the lead on your bill, or that legislator's staff person.

## Staff in Legislatures

Most senior staff members in legislatures, and even some who are not so senior, wield enormous behind-the-scenes power. The ability of your lobbyist to develop a good working relationship with the legislative staff person assigned to your bill is almost as important as your selection of the legislator who will lead your effort. Staff people can be very useful to your organization. They can help you (1) become familiar with the other members of the committee and their staffs, (2) know who among them should be targeted to support the bill early in the process, (3) know which legislators' staffs will help and which ones will not, (4) obtain regular updates on where committee members stand on your bill, (5) know what actions would be helpful from your grass roots and when, (6) show you how to get the most out of hearings on your measure, and (7) obtain information on how to get legislative-report language that strengthens your bill. They can also help you with much more. You, of course, will be developing information on key members of the legislature from other sources as well. By cross-checking that information with a legislative staff person who is taking the lead on your bill, you can greatly improve the targeting of all your efforts.

For your part, there are a number of ways in which you can be helpful to your legislative staff person in moving your legislation forward. You can offer to draft a statement that his or her boss can use in conducting hearings on your bill or in getting ready to speak on your measure before a group. After a committee votes favorably to move your bill out of committee, you can also offer to help develop draft language for the report on the legislation. A committee report includes information on the committee's findings and recommendations. The opportunity to draft such a statement helps you ensure that your group's views will be appropriately included. The key point is that you should be alert to the many ways in which you can offer to help the legislative staff person move your bill, by offering to take on some of the necessary writing or other staff work.

Over time, you will get a sense of how much the staff person will be willing to help. Because of the extraordinary number of hours they may spend on a measure, staff people often develop commitment to the legislation that is even greater than their bosses' commitment. Such commitment can help significantly in moving your legislation. Keep in mind, however, that the legislator has the final say, and that keeping his or her commitment strong is crucial. Regardless of how strongly a staff person feels about your bill, he or she won't be able to win the day for you if the legislator is willing to trade your bill for another.

You will want to find a way of recognizing staff people who have been especially helpful. Presenting a plaque, or offering similar recognition, before an appropriate group is one way. But remember that the most important public recognition should always go to the legislator.

Perhaps it goes without saying that trust is absolutely central to building a strong relationship with staff people. Keeping commitments to staff people to hold information in confidence is crucial, as difficult as it may be sometimes. Not only is it right to do so, but you won't get a second chance if you slip up.

Most nonprofits that lobby don't start by learning the legislative process, nor should they. Most begin by doing what they already know how to do with great effectiveness. They write letters, they telephone, or perhaps they even visit their legislators, to let lawmakers know how particular legislative proposals will affect their organizations' services. It's not that knowing the lobbying process isn't helpful; someone in your organization should know at least a few of the basics. It's important, however, not to get entangled by trying to achieve complete mastery of the labyrinthine legislative process before you take action. Keep your eye on the target, and on the thing that nonprofits do best: telling your organization's story effectively to your legislators. If some try to convince you that you must master all the intricacies of the legislative process before taking action on legislation, remind them that Irving Berlin never stopped to learn to read or write music.

If you are new to lobbying, remember that there is no one right or wrong way to lobby. There are as many ways to lobby as there are people who do it. Remember, too, that you won't learn to lobby by reading this book or any other. You learn to do it by doing it.

## Lobbying the Administration

Actions of the executive branch of government, such as the issuing of regulations that spell out the intent of legislation, can profoundly affect programs supported by nonprofits. It is possible for an administration at any level of government to modify legislation so greatly that truth is lent to the old adage "What the legislature gives through legislation, the administration takes away through regulation."

Often, the regulations proposed by an executive agency will change the original purposes of legislation so greatly that nonprofits must fight every bit as hard to change the regulations as they did to enact the measure in the first place. For example, the regulations proposed in late 1986 by the Internal Revenue Service to implement the 1976 lobby law were so restrictive and ambiguous that they threatened to end lobbying by most nonprofits. Only after a grueling four-month battle, in which nonprofits lobbied administration officials and enlisted the support of Congress, did the IRS agree to consider drafting new regulations. Superb *lobbying* regulations governing the 1976 law were ultimately issued by the IRS in 1990.

Nonprofits may lobby an administration for a variety of reasons: seeking changes in regulations, encouraging an administration to propose legislation or appropriations, or urging an administration to support a measure being considered by a legislature. Regardless of the reasons, the lobbying techniques, including the involvement of legislative volunteer networks, are very similar to those used in lobbying a legislature, and they are neither difficult nor complex. Anyone who can write a letter or make a telephone call can effectively lobby an administration for a policy change, through contacting the administration directly or through contacting members of the legislature and urging them to ask the administration to support the measure.

Staff people in the executive branch are not always responsive to lobbying by nonprofits. For example, the staff responsible for drafting IRS regulations and other policies are often civil service personnel, not political appointees. Therefore, they are not very vulnerable to pressures from the grass roots. Often, however, staff members are open to reason when they are presented with arguments about how proposed regulations will negatively affect programs supported by the nonprofits. If the people in an executive agency who are ultimately responsible for regulations are not willing to make changes, then nonprofits have to find other avenues to get the administration to make modifications.

### Enlisting the Help of the Legislature

Success in changing proposed regulations usually requires your lobbying the executive (president, governor, mayor) and/or the heads of executive departments or agencies who are *appointed* by the chief executive and have reason to be more responsive to grassroots pressures, such as that from legislative networks. At the federal level, effective lobbying of the administration almost always involves enlisting the help of members of Congress.

Members of Congress resent having their legislation modified by regulations in ways that they or their constituents think are not consistent with original legislative intent. Enlisting the support of the chair and other members of the appropriate legislative committee can be critically important in mobilizing support for modifying the regulations. At the same time, staff people in an executive agency that has drafted the regulations are interested in maintaining good relationshps with the chair and other members of the committee responsible for enacting the legislation. After all, committee members usually have the power to affect the well-being—often including the appropriations—of the agency that developed the regulations. Enlisting large numbers of other legislators can also help greatly in moving the administration to modify or drop proposed regulations. In any case, the point is that legislators have much more power than nonprofits do to influence an administration. By all means, enlist them in your efforts. In the 1987 battle with the IRS over the regulations governing lobbying by nonprofits, it was finally the involvement of Senators Moynihan (D-N.Y.), Packwood (R-Or.), DeConcini (D-Ariz.), and D'Amato (R-N.Y.) and of Congressmen Rostenkowski (D-Ill.), Rangel (D-N.Y.), and Vander Jagt (R-Minn.)—all key members of committees that have jurisdiction over the IRS or authority for its appropriations—that played the pivotal role in getting the agency to reconsider its regulations.

If you have enlisted the support of a key legislator to help you get an administration to change proposed regulations, make a special effort to develop a good working relationship with the legislator's congressional staff person. Staff people know that nonprofits can help mobilize constituents to support their bosses' efforts. They play a pivotal, behind-the-scenes role in providing up-to-the-minute information, circulating "Dear Colleague" letters, assisting with hearings, and making their bosses available to meet with nonprofits as an encouragement to lobbying efforts. Keep in mind that senior staff people almost always know what actions by members of Congress will have the greatest impact on the administration. Look to them for suggestions regarding strategy.

### Getting the Press's Support

Getting press support for your position, and press criticism of the government's position, can also have an enormous impact. News stories, editorials, op-ed pieces, letters to the editor in support of your position on regulations or other administrative initiatives—all of these will help get the attention of any administration. Simply getting press coverage will not win your issue. But press coverage, along with grass-roots lobbying, lobbying of the administration by influential members of your nonprofit, and most important, the support of legislators, will often generate the strength you need for the change you seek.

# 3

# Effective Communications:
# The Key to Mobilizing
# Your Lobbying Strength

Unlike many other lobbying groups, a nonprofit organization's power does not come from contributions to a legislator's campaign (that's prohibited). It comes from well-informed members who recognize the value of encouraging legislators to support the nonprofit's legislative issues. While they cannot contribute dollars to a legislator, nonprofits are nevertheless important to him or her because they constitute an important force in the community by virtue of both the quality and the number of their members. Legislators are particularly sensitive to groups from their home districts, since such groups are composed of the legislator's constituents, and their members go to the polls. The key question is how you can communicate with your organization's members so that they will contact their legislators on behalf of the group's concerns.

Many nonprofits rely completely on written communications to move their members to action. They fail to recognize that if written communications were followed up with telephone calls, the organization would greatly multiply the number of contacts its members make with legislators. Most of us find it all too easy to put aside written communications that request us to take action, especially if the action involves writing a letter or calling a legislator. Our intentions are good; we plan to do it in a day or two, but somehow that day never comes. We have to give time and thought to the communication, and we are not completely sure how to go about it. If we are called, however—if there is a person on the other end of the line urging us to act on the request—we are much more likely to do it.

Telephone follow-up is time-consuming and can be costly, but the increased contacts repay the investment of time and money. Moreover, those who phone always receive valuable information from the key volunteers to whom they are speaking, through the give-and-take of a conversation. Furthermore, those who make the calls almost always find the process itself energizing, given the camaraderie that develops between the callers and those who are being asked to make the contacts.

Many organizations cut the costs of telephoning by setting up a telephone tree, whereby one person calls five people, and each of those five calls five more, and so on. Regardless of how you do it, it is critically important that you make calls to urge response to your action alerts. You may be inclined to mail your alert to members and others, hoping that will be enough to generate the action you want. Resist that impulse. Telephoning is hard work, but it often makes the difference between success and failure.

In any communication with your members, accuracy counts. If a member of your organization uses inaccurate information that she received from you when she communicates with a legislator, everyone loses. The legislator loses because accuracy is critically important to all that he or she does. Few things can be more embarrassing to a legislator than to have used erroneous information. Your group's member loses credibility with the legislator, and you lose credibility with your member. If you inadvertently send inaccurate information to your members, always correct it as quickly as possible, painful as that may be.

It is difficult but important to try to keep your legislative alert (your explanation of the issue and the action needed) to one sheet, front and back. If you must send more information, attach supplemental briefing materials. Nothing dampens a contact person's enthusiasm more quickly than receiving a legislative alert that calls for quick action but obliges the recipient to wade through four or five pages to get the necessary information. Be certain that your first paragraph tells the reader what the issue is and what action is needed. Word your alert so that it accomplishes that end. You will have to work at it, but you risk losing the reader if he or she doesn't get the main message first.

Don't use legislative jargon in your alert. It may take a few more words to convey what a mark-up is, but why use the term if you're not absolutely certain that all your readers know that a mark-up is a committee making its final changes in legislation?

Keep your alert self-contained, so that the reader doesn't have to refer to an earlier alert (they have probably discarded it). Don't make assumptions about how much your readers know from your past communications with them. In the heat of a key legislative fight, you are living with the issue twenty-four hours a day, but they are not. They cannot make an intelligent contact if your alert does not provide any background information, even though it may be redundant for some readers.

Just to be doubly certain that your alert is clear, ask several others in your office, who are not as close to the issue as you are, to read it for clarity. If you are fortunate enough to have interns, they can be particularly helpful, because they probably will be relatively new to the subject and therefore can read the alert for clarity from an outsider's point of view.

Be certain that your communications are mailed soon enough for your members to contact their legislators. Nothing makes your organization look worse (to say nothing of hurting your cause) than mailing your alert too late for action. It is important to know how quickly mail usually reaches your members. If you have any doubt about the time necessary to reach people by mail, use the telephone, or send telegrams to get your message to your members.

Because timeliness is so important, most charities now use photocopying rather than commercial printing for their legislative alerts. The minute you get the okay on the final version of your alert, you should be able to duplicate it. It makes no sense to lose a day or two while a printer gets around to doing the job. A photocopied alert may not look as impressive as a printed one, but what will impress your readers most will be the fact that they received it with plenty of time for action.

## Feedback and Records

Encourage your members always to send you copies of any correspondence that they have received from legislators. Nonprofits' members are notoriously derelict in this area, but keep after them. All replies, even those that are noncommital, tell you something about the legislator's position.

If you are seeking cosponsors for your legislation, regularly send your members a list of all legislators and indicate who has already signed on. Your members will check the list to see if their legislators are cosponsors and will know whether they need to get in touch with them. Regular updates also keep your members involved by showing them the results of their efforts.

## Tallies of Support

It is very important to keep a confidential support tally that gives your judgments regarding legislators' positions. This list could be coded as follows:

> S = supports
> LTS = leaning toward support
> U = undecided
> LAS = leaning against support
> A = against

It is also important to remember that these judgments are often subjective, since they are pieced together from information that may have a variety of sources. Such a list should *not* be sent out to your members. A person who sees that her legislator is leaning against support of your measure may write to the legislator and ask why he or she is not supporting it, even though the "leaning against" designation is simply a judgment that you made, and it may not be altogether accurate. The legislator probably will be unhappy, to say the least, about receiving a communication that does not accurately reflect his or her position. This misunderstanding may damage the relationship between your member and the legislator, and between your member and you.

Even though such a list must be treated with caution, it can still be very important to your group's leaders and to the legislator who is leading the effort on your measure. The legislator will need regular updates of your assessment of support for the measure. On the basis of the tally, you can selectively urge your members to make special contacts with legislators who are not supportive, taking care to communicate those legislators' positions in such a way that your volunteers can act without jeopardizing relationships.

### Frequency of Alerts

Legislative alerts should be sent out as often as necessary, which may mean three times in one month and not at all for the next several months. Some nonprofits send out government relations updates at designated times each month, even if there is little to report. There are those who argue that sending a government relations update on a regular schedule develops a readership, but that is not likely to happen if you are stretching to fill up the space. You will soon lose your readers' interest and their possible supportive actions unless you are reporting something worthy of their time.

### Staying with the Process

Major legislative changes often take five to six years to achieve, and it is sometimes difficult to keep members motivated for that long. It is important to be candid from the start about the time that may be required. You should also emphasize that persistence ranks close to the top, if it is not at the top, of any list of attributes essential to a successful legislative effort. There's no magic to success, just perseverance and hard work.

# 4

# Developing
# Grassroots Action
# Through a Legislative Network

"All politics is local," according to former Speaker of the House Thomas "Tip" O'Neill. That's why effective lobbying by nonprofits requires a legislative network.

The central mission of a network is empowerment—helping people know how and when to take action on issues important to them and those they seek to serve. Legislative networks are time-consuming to organize. They require thoughtful attention to maintain, are not very glamorous, and are therefore easy to neglect. But remember, as John F. Kennedy said, "Things don't just happen. They're made to happen." That's what legislative networks do.

It is a well-known fact that communications from the grass roots do have an important impact on decisions in any legislature. Legislative staff people repeatedly emphasize that those back-home contacts are often the determining factor in how their bosses vote on an issue. But somehow we tend to be slow to believe this fact and slower still to act on it. Well-informed contacts by nonprofit volunteers are at the heart of almost every successful legislative effort, and that volunteer action is best mobilized through a legislative network.

Each nonprofit's legislative network is different from the next, because nonprofits have vastly different organizational structures. But all legislative networks have one thing in common: an organized, systematic means of communicating on short notice with network volunteers who have agreed to contact their legislators on behalf of legislation backed by the nonprofits.

To start, the network doesn't have to be elaborate. It can consist of only one network volunteer, in each of the key legislative districts represented on the committee(s) that will be considering your bill. Later, according to need, the network can be expanded to all the districts represented on these committees and, ultimately, to the whole legislature. But don't worry about organizing a network to cover all legislators at the outset. Instead, concentrate on establishing a sound network for those key members of the legislature who will have the greatest influence on the outcome of your bill.

It is important that your network be composed of volunteers, rather than the paid staff members of a nonprofit. If you select influential volunteers, their contacts, in most cases, will have a far greater impact on legislators than will the contacts of staff people. Because they are contributing their time, volunteers are also often perceived by legislators and their staffs to have less monetary interest in outcomes, and so their contacts have more credibility.

To set up a network, you simply need to make a list of those legislators whom you want to contact, delineate the geographical district covered by each legislator, recruit volunteers who live in the appropriate districts and have (or can establish) relationships with those legislators, and develop a means of communicating quickly with all the members of your network.

The information that you will need about each legislator to pass on to your network volunteers will include his or her political party, address in the capital, address in the legislative district, and telephone number. If available, you will also want the names of legislative staff people who will be assigned to your issue. While it is not crucial, it is helpful to include information on how legislators have voted on past issues of concern to your organization. Biographical information also helps. If you want several pages of biographical information on a member of Congress, it is available in the latest edition of Duncan (1989).

It is important to recruit network volunteers who really have a commitment to your issue and who have staying power. Since it often takes a number of years to pass major legislation, commitment is important. Even the best relationship with a legislator is of little value if a volunteer is not going to work aggressively to gain the legislator's support, or if he loses interest when your bill does not show quick movement in the legislature.

It helps to recruit network volunteers who are known to and respected by the legislators and who live in their districts. This is the first criterion. If a volunteer doesn't know a legislator, try to make certain that the volunteer does have the capacity for developing a strong relationship.

The best way to be certain that your network volunteer will be effective is to have firsthand knowledge of that person. That isn't always possible, but others whom you trust may know someone who would be right for the job. You can also send a mailing to your members, asking for volunteers for the legislative network. Volunteers can be asked to provide information about the strength of their contacts with legislators. Initially, you may be less certain that volunteers recruited by mail will follow through effectively on their responsibilities, but your experience over time with this group will tell you whom you can count on and should retain.

The principal job of network volunteers is to contact legislators on behalf of your issues. Their second responsibility, equally important, is to mobilize support by others in their communities. In many cases, network volunteers will be active with local chapters of your organization or with other groups, whose members can be recruited to support your legislation. It is very important for network volunteers to know that, at the very minimum, they are responsible for contacting legislators and reporting to you on those contacts, but it will help greatly to strengthen your impact if volunteers also agree to recruit others.

To have impact, network volunteers have to be able to provide sound, timely information to their legislators. Most nonprofits send action alerts to their network volunteers to provide that information, and the most effective groups *always* follow up the alert with a telephone call.

Your ability to generate contacts will be greatly increased if you follow up your action alerts with telephone calls. Some groups set up telephone "trees," where one person calls five people who then call an additional five, and so on. Other nonprofits set up a telephone "bank" in their office, where volunteers and/or staff call

all network volunteers directly. Others use a combination. The key
is to find a method of telephoning which is as foolproof as possible
in the sense of assuring that the calls are made. Without the calls,
you will lose much of the impact of your action alerts. The temptation, because telephoning can be so time-consuming, is simply to
send the action alert and then just hope for the best. Don't do it.
Make the calls.

It is, of course, vital that the action alert arrive in time for
the volunteers to write the letter or call the legislator prior to action
on your bill. Don't depend on your nonprofit's newsletter or bulletin to get the action from your volunteers. First off, chances are
that it will not reach the people in the field at the time when the
information is needed, and, in any case, publications that cover a
wide variety of issues of concern to the organization do not convey
the same sense of urgency and importance that separate legislative
action alerts do. However, your organization's newsletter or bulletin
can provide an effective supplement to your action alerts by giving
a general update on the progress of the legislation.

Your action alert should state in the first sentence or two
what action is needed. Don't leave out key information because it
was in past alerts; it might have been forgotten or the alert discarded. Urge network volunteers to include illustrative anecdotes or
other specific information in their contacts with legislators which
show firsthand how the legislator's constituents will be affected by
the vote on your issue. Ask volunteers always to thank legislators
for their vote. It is the right thing to do and the legislator and the
legislator's staff will remember it.

Most nonprofits have several groups within their memberships that they reach out to for legislative action. They have primary networks of volunteers specifically designated to contact
particular legislators. Most organizations, however, consider their
total memberships to be part of their legislative networks. On issues
of major importance, they try to mobilize action on the part of all
members. Boards of directors and key committees should also be
considered special networks, to be turned to on selected occasions.

When working with smaller groups, such as your nonprofit's
board, you should get information about which legislators the
members may know personally and about the strength of those

contacts. It is far more difficult to get this kind of information from every member of the organization, but some nonprofits have been able to do so by polling members.

Boards, committees, other groups in your organization and the total membership can increase your organization's legislative impact substantially. Before organizing other groups, however, be certain that your primary network is in place and working well.

## Keeping Your Network Alive

Legislative networks often do not remain effective over time. Some nonprofits are not really convinced that networks are where the power to effect legislative change resides, or they realize it but do not understand how necessary commitment and hard work are in keeping a network alive and effective. Once a network is in place, there is often an inclination to consider the job done and go on to other, more interesting activities, such as meetings with legislators or their staffs. But thinking about the network only when action is needed won't work. To remain strong, a legislative network needs to be asked regularly to take action. Members must be kept up-to-date on what's happening with their legislation, even when action isn't required, and they need to be thanked, regularly and thoughtfully, for their work.

I disagree with those who hold that networks should be asked to take action only once or twice a year, for fear of wearing them out. The reverse is true. Networks atrophy because they are too seldom called on to do anything. As a result, they get the unstated message that they are not needed. It is important to ask for action only when it is really needed, but on any major legislative issue, that will be more than once or twice a year.

You can take several steps, in addition to asking for action, that will help keep volunteers as part of the team. Most important is that they get regular brief updates on where the legislation stands. If you can, also invite your network's members to come to the capital and receive updates from the legislators leading your effort. They can make calls on their legislators while in the capital and meet with your group's top leaders.

Saying "thank you" is both right and important. Finding a way of saying it to a large group in a sincere way is difficult. Making telephone calls is one effective way of conveying special thanks that won't sound "canned." If it's worth your time to call network volunteers and urge them to take action on legislation, then it is certainly worth the time and expense to call them occasionally with updates and thanks. A letter sometimes conveys the message, although most volunteers recognize a mass-mailed letter produced by a word processor, even if the letter is personally signed. You may want to express your thanks in a legislative alert, but make your thanks special by having the legislator who is leading your effort formulate the statement. (You can probably formulate the statement for the legislator and get it approved through your staff contact.) In addition, publicly state your volunteer leaders' names in your organization's newsletter or in a similar publication.

To find out whether your network is working, make inquiries of staff people who should be hearing from your grass roots. They will let you know how much they are hearing on your issue. If it turns out that some volunteers are not doing the job, it is important to thank them and find replacements.

### Keeping Up-To-Date Information

One side benefit of calling network volunteers to action is that you turn up new information that can help you know how to target your future efforts. Be sure that the person telephoning the volunteers records any new information regarding legislators' positions. Equally important, also record any information that indicates how network volunteers are doing their jobs. Over time, you will develop a list of network volunteers who are especially responsive. They will become a select group that you will call first, because they can be counted on to take quick action. Their responsiveness almost always helps motivate the people who phone volunteers to be enthusiastic in the rest of their contacts.

Some nonprofits keep information about their network volunteers in computer files available on printouts. Such files include names, addresses, telephone numbers, and brief summaries of information from past contacts with the volunteers. This information is especially helpful if a new staff person is phoning volunteers. You don't need a computer to keep the information (although a computer makes it easier). A simple list of volunteers, with basic information and space to keep handwritten summaries of contacts, is all that is essential.

# 5

# How to
# Communicate Effectively
# with Legislators

There have been a number of studies on which communications count most in influencing a legislator's point of view. Don't rely too much on survey findings. The most effective method will be the one that, over time, works best for your group. Personal visits, thoughtful letters from constituents, site visits (where a legislator sees firsthand the needs your group is trying to meet), and telephone calls from constituents whom the legislator respects—all of these can be highly effective. On balance, a personal visit from an influential constituent is clearly better than a letter or a phone call from the same constituent, and one site visit would probably be better than ten personal visits or one-hundred letters or phone calls. You will develop your own sense of what works best. Your own experience will be a far better guide than any study, although studies can provide some useful general direction for your work.

A study by the Institute for Government Public Information (Burson-Marsteller, 1981) provides important information about which sources of communications congressional staff rated as most effective. Staff people's views are important because of the enormous influence that staffers exert on the members of Congress for whom they work. There were several major findings of the study. First, spontaneous, individually composed letters from constituents were seen as the most effective way of communicating with congressional decision makers. These letters received more attention than any other form of written communication. Nevertheless, orchestrated mail also received surprisingly high ratings, while still rated as less effective than spontaneous letters. Second, for all types of issues, the preferred communication sources are letters, phone calls, and visits from constituents; the press (news articles and editorials in national and local daily newspapers); and governmental information sources (the Congressional Research Service, the *Congressional Record*, and other government publications). Other findings are shown in Table 1. An earlier study (Barry, 1977) asked representatives of eighty-three public interest groups their opinions of various communication sources. Table 2 shows the results of that study.

Letter writing, the lobbying technique most used by nonprofits, ranks first or second in these two surveys. Regardless of which means of communication you use, there are a few general guidelines and tips that will help you make your point with legislators.

Perhaps the most important thing you need to know is your subject. What is the substance of the legislation? Why is it important? What will happen if it passes? What will be the consequences if it fails? How much will it cost? Most important, what will be the impact of the legislation on the legislator's constituents? It is particularly helpful to give an illustration or two of how the problem will affect the legislator's district, but don't feel that you have to become an expert on the subject before you make the communication. Just be sure of the facts that you report, and build your communication around them.

It helps to know at least a little about your legislator, and Duncan (1989) is one good source of detailed information on the individual members of Congress, including positions they have taken, their interest group rating and their education, occupation, and so on. However, don't let any lack of detailed knowledge about your legislators stand in your way. Legislators pay attention to well-presented positions by constituents regardless of whether the presenters tie in the points they are making with personal knowledge about legislators.

In all communications, whether by phone calls, letters, or personal meetings, it is important to be accurate, brief, clear and timely, as already discussed. No matter how much you will some-

Table 1. Highest-Ranked Sources of Communication.

| Rank | Method | Avg. Rank |
|------|--------|-----------|
| 1. | Spontaneous letters from constituents | 1.67 |
| 2. | Telephone calls from constituents | 3.67 |
| 3. | Congressional Research Service | 4.00 |
| 4. | Articles in major daily newspapers | 5.00 |
| 5. | Editorials in major daily newspapers | 7.00 |
| 6. | Visits from constituents | 7.67 |
| 7. | Articles in district daily newspapers | 7.67 |
| 8. | *Congressional Record* | 8.33 |
| 9. | Editorials in district daily newspapers | 8.67 |
| 10. | Government publications | 11.67 |
| 11. | Orchestrated mail from constituents | 12.67 |
| 12. | Op-ed/opinion pieces in major daily newspapers | 13.00 |
| 13. | Op-ed/opinion pieces in local daily newspapers | 16.00 |
| 14. | Spontaneous letters from state officials | 16.33 |
| 15. | Spontaneous letters from interest groups | 16.33 |
| 16. | Telephone calls from friends | 19.33 |
| 17. | Telephone calls from state opinion leaders | 20.33 |
| 18. | Spontaneous letters from Congressional leaders | 20.67 |
| 19. | Visits from paid lobbyists | 21.67 |
| 20. | Position papers, mailed information kits | 21.67 |
| 21. | Phone calls from interest groups | 23.33 |
| 22. | Invitations to speak | 24.67 |
| 23. | Petitions from constituents | 25.00 |
| 24. | Phone calls from state officials | 25.00 |
| 25. | Articles in national news magazines | 25.00 |
| 26. | Interest groups' mailed newsletters | 25.33 |
| 27. | National television news | 26.00 |
| 28. | Visits from Washington reps | 27.33 |
| 29. | Editorials in district weekly newspapers | 34.00 |
| 30. | News articles in district weekly newspapers | 36.67 |

*Source:* Adapted from Burson-Marsteller (1981).

times want to, never become angry or argumentative with your legislator about his or her failure to support your position. You will almost certainly have to go back to that same legislator sometime in the future. If you have strained your relationship by getting angry—no matter how much you may have been justified in doing so—chances are that you won't get through the door. If you do, your information may be largely discounted.

In addition to these general guidelines, there are more specific tips that may help you. Since these tips cover far more infor-

Table 2. Effectiveness of Communication Tactics.

| Source of Communication | Very Effective/ Effective (in Percentages)[a] | Not Effective |
|---|---|---|
| Personal presentation | 53 | 7 |
| Letter writing | 47 | 4 |
| Contact by influential member or constituent | 34 | 1 |
| Release of research | 30 | 6 |
| Litigation | 29 | 5 |
| Public relations | 24 | — |
| Testimony at congressional hearings | 20 | 42 |
| Published voter records | 18 | 4 |
| Contributions of money | 8 | — |
| Political demonstrations | 8 | 5 |

[a]Figures represent percentages of respondents.
*Source:* Adapted from Barry (1977).

mation than you will need, just skim through them, see what fits for you, and ignore the rest.

## Letters

Nonprofit organizations rely greatly on mail campaigns to persuade legislators to support positions. Whether you are organizing a mail campaign or writing just one letter from your organization, it is important to keep in mind that the competition is stiff. More than two hundred million pieces of mail are sent to Congress each year, so give careful thought to your letter. (Table 3 shows proper forms of address to be used with various state and federal officials.)

If you know the legislator, make that clear in the first paragraph. This will alert the person opening the mail to give the letter special attention. By all means, use the legislator's first name if you have established that kind of relationship, and sign it with your first name.

Write on plain stationery or on your personal or business letterhead. Some legislators downgrade the importance of a letter if they think it has been motivated by an organization as part of a

**Table 3. Proper Forms of Address.**

| Person Addressed | | Salutation | Complimentary Close |
|---|---|---|---|
| President of the United States | The President<br>The White House<br>Washington, D.C.<br>20500 | Dear Mr. President: | Sincerely yours, |
| U.S. Senator | The Honorable ____<br>United States Senate<br>Washington, D.C.<br>20510 | Dear Senator ____ : | Sincerely yours, |
| U.S. Representative | The Honorable ____<br>United States House<br>of Representatives<br>Washington, D.C.<br>20515 | Dear Mr./Ms. ____ : | Sincerely yours, |
| | The Honorable ____<br>Governor of ____ | Dear Governor ____ : | Sincerely yours, |
| | The Honorable ____<br>House of<br>Representatives<br>State Capitol | Dear Mr./Ms. ____ : | Sincerely yours, |
| | The Honorable ____<br>The State Senate<br>State Capitol | Dear Senator ____ : | Sincerely yours, |

campaign. Do, however, mention your nonprofit group if you are fairly certain that it will strengthen the impact of your letter.

Handwritten letters are fine, as long as they are legible. They often get more attention than typed letters. (Legislators know that a machine cannot produce a handwritten letter.)

Keep your letter to one page. Put it in your own words, avoid buzz words or jargon, and use only those acronyms that you are very certain the legislator will know. Cover only one issue per letter. In the first paragraph, ask for the action that you want your legislator to take. Send enclosures if you think more information is needed. Relevant editorials and news stories from local papers in the legislator's district will get his or her attention. Identify the legislation clearly, with the bill number of the legislation if you know it, and sign your letter over your typed or printed name.

Ask the legislator to reply, and ask very directly whether he or she will support your position. Legislators are masters of non-replies—that is, letters that avoid giving you their positions. To smoke out his or her position, be as direct as possible while still being courteous. Like everyone else, legislators dislike a threatening tone. Chances are excellent that your legislator will be very aware of the political fallout of not voting for your proposal, and so it serves no useful purpose to even hint about it. Keep in mind the old saying that you catch more flies with honey than you do with vinegar.

Be certain that the legislator's name is spelled correctly and that the address is right. Envelopes get detached, so put your return address on the letter. Be certain that your legislator receives the letter before the vote.

Thank the legislator. Legislative staffers repeatedly say that legislators seldom receive thanks. Sending your thanks is the right thing to do and is a great way to strengthen a relationship. But also write to let the legislator know if you disapprove of the way he or she has voted. That will get attention, too.

Provide copies of any replies you receive to the leaders and government relations committee of your nonprofit. It is useful to keep them up-to-date on where the legislator stands and on whether to keep pressure on him or her.

Don't overstate your nonprofit's influence; it will only detract from your message. Do let your legislator know the size and mission of your group, however. Legislators are very aware of how much attention to pay to almost every group in their districts, so don't overstate—or understate. Just give the facts.

Send letters only to your own legislator, unless you are the president of a group with members from other legislative districts. Even then, it is well to keep in mind that legislators tend to pay only limited attention to mail from outside their districts.

There have been mixed reviews of postcards, sample letters, and similar communications produced in centrally organized efforts to mobilize grass-roots support on issues. Some discount the impact of postcards and "canned" letters. Others hold that they can be helpful. As Common Cause (1979) advises, any letter is better than none. That's good advice.

## Personal Visits

Personal meetings with constituents are very highly ranked among effective ways of communicating with legislators. The first time you meet your legislator face to face, you may be nervous; it would be unusual if you were not. Keep in mind, however, that legislators are almost always very eager to win your support. They want to put their best foot forward with their constituents, and they are sincerely interested in getting their constituents' views on legislation. Remember that you are the expert on the subject—you have information that the legislator needs. Legislators and their staff people repeatedly say that the information nonprofits provide is important to their decisions, so don't feel that you are entering the legislator's office as a supplicant.

There will be many reasons why your group may want to meet with a legislator who is taking a leadership role on your bill. During the visit, don't miss the opportunity to seek advice on how your organization can be most helpful in developing support for your legislation. Remember that you will think of the bill you are supporting as your legislation, but the legislator will naturally consider it to be his or her bill and will have a number of ideas and suggestions to help you focus your efforts.

If you have decided to meet with your legislator, there are ways to help the meeting run smoothly. It is important to make an appointment, if at all possible. It is better to telephone than to write for the appointment, because calling makes it easier to find an acceptable date. It is also more difficult for the appointments secretary to turn you down by telephone than by letter. It is always more effective if you as a constituent ask for an appointment, rather than having your organization's staff make that contact.

If you don't have an appointment and the legislator is on the floor of the House or the Senate, as a last resort—and only if it is critically important—send in a note by House or Senate page, asking that the legislator come out to speak with you. Use this approach only if you know the legislator well enough to be confident that the interruption won't hurt your cause more than help it.

Legislators almost always do try to meet with their constituents. Don't turn down the opportunity to meet with a staffer, however, if it develops that the legislator cannot meet your schedule. In Congress, senior staff people wield considerable power and often are able to give more time and attention to issues than legislators can. Representatives and senators maintain district offices, and meetings there can be particularly productive because legislators usually are less harried when they are home on weekends or during recesses.

It is acceptable to assemble a delegation for the meeting. It may be a small group of three or four, but it is all right to take as many as fifteen or twenty. Small meetings may allow for more detailed discussion of an issue, including frank comments from the legislator about the dilemma he or she faces in making choices on the issue.

One delegate should be designated as the principal spokesperson. The group should meet at least briefly in advance, to orchestrate the visit. Be certain that there is agreement on the objectives to be accomplished in the meeting and on the points to be stressed.

Having more than one person presenting information permits a person who is not talking to the legislator to be ready to step in with the next key point, but don't overpower your legislator. Present your views with conviction, but don't put him or her on the defensive.

You will probably know considerably more about your subject than your legislator does, so there is no reason to feel abashed. Legislators will welcome information and will particularly appreciate any anecdotes or illustrations that spell out what the impact will be on people in their legislative districts.

It helps to cover your issue from the legislator's perspective, tying it in with his or her past votes or interests. Listen attentively. Often, the legislator's opening discussion with you will give you clues about how to connect your issue with his or her concerns.

If you don't have the answer to a legislator's question, say so. Don't bluff. Tell the legislator that you will provide the information, and then be certain that you do.

Give responses to arguments that you know your opposition will raise, but don't degrade your opponents. They believe in their cause as strongly as you believe in yours. It is important to provide information, both orally and in a fact sheet that you leave with the legislator. Be certain that it includes a brief description of your issue, why it is important to your organization, and the action that you want the legislator to take. Have a fact sheet for the legislative aide as well. The aide may be your principal contact in the future, so be certain to strengthen that contact during the visit.

After the visit, write a letter of thanks to the legislator. Remind him or her of any agreements reached, and provide any information that you promised.

### Testimony

Testimony ranks low on the list of effective ways to communicate with legislators, but it is important to know how to give it. Legislative bodies call for public hearings for a number of reasons. They may be held to inform the public about issues or to get the information they need in helping to draft laws or in finding out whether a law is needed. Hearings may also be scheduled as "window dressing" for decisions that have already been made.

At the very least, providing testimony—even when it is given in hearings of questionable value—serves the useful purpose of requiring a group to develop a fairly comprehensive statement of its position. Sound testimony can help to establish your organization as an authority in your field. It can also provide useful quotations for speeches and publications. In that way, testimony can be helpful to a nonprofit, even if hearings are perfunctory. In deciding whether to testify, remember that a decision against testifying sends a message to the legislators that your organization is not interested or, worse, that you have reasons to avoid questions on the subject.

If you are planning to present testimony, keep your statement brief, and always provide a one-page summary as the initial page of your written testimony. Legislators usually don't read testimony, and staffers often only scan it. Providing a summary helps ensure that your main points will be noted. Most legislative bodies have format requirements for testimony, including the number of copies you should have and when they should be delivered to the committee. The cover page of your statement should include the legislative committee before which you are testifying; the name, title, and organization of the person testifying; and the date. A written request is almost always required from a person who wishes to testify before Congress.

At congressional hearings, witnesses are usually asked to keep oral statements to under five minutes, although a longer statement will be accepted for the record. Oral statements should not be read word by word. They should be given as much as possible from brief outlines that permit presenters to maintain eye contact with committee members. If you can't answer a question, it is perfectly acceptable to say that you don't have the information but will get it for the committee immediately.

The quality of your organization's statement is important, but the skill of the presenter is equally important in making a favorable impression for your cause. Testimony should be presented by a high-ranking well-informed volunteer. The chief staff officer or other staff members can accompany the volunteer, to help answer questions. The second-best choice is for the chief staff officer to present the testimony, but that choice diminishes the citizen-based impact of the statement.

It is helpful to know in advance which committee members are likely to be present and whether they will be friendly. That information is often available from the staff of the legislator who supports your position. Plant questions with friendly legislators who you know will be at the hearing, so that you can get those questions and your answers into the public record. It is usually easy to do this by working with legislative staff members. If there will be witnesses unfriendly to your cause, anticipate the opposing arguments they will make, and provide responses to friendly legislators. You can also provide questions to friendly legislators, which they can raise with unfriendly witness, to make points for you.

You may get questions that seem hostile. It is perfectly acceptable to be direct in your responses, but always be courteous. If a legislator seems particularly hostile, make a special point of trying to see him or her later, or follow up your testimony with a letter that deals with the issues he or she has raised.

If your organization is working closely with the chair of the committee holding the hearings, it is acceptable to ask staffers if they would like to have your group draft the opening statement for the chair. Staff people often welcome such statements as a starting point for the drafts they ultimately present to chairpersons.

Finally, get other groups to sign on to your testimony if they are not planning to testify separately. Having several other organizations that are well known to legislators sign on to your testimony can significantly strengthen the impact of the statement.

At the very least, hearings provide a public record that can be the springboard for major legislative changes. Two sets of hearings that affected nonprofits serve as superb examples. In 1975, the House Ways and Means Committee conducted hearings on proposed legislation to broaden and clarify the rights of charities to lobby. The public record established at the hearing—on the basis of testimony from a wide variety of experts, the U.S. Department of the Treasury, and members of Congress—was indispensable to the success of later lobbying efforts. These culminated in the enactment of very enlightened legislation governing lobbying by nonprofits.

Public hearings were also of enormous importance in the final enactment of the charitable deduction for people who do not itemize their tax returns. During the hearings, conducted in January 1980, testimony was received from fifty-nine individuals representing the arts, education, environmental concerns, religion, health, welfare, advocacy organizations, international issues, and many more areas. The hearings heightened the visibility of the issue, both in Congress and in the media, and helped set the stage for enactment of the legislation in 1981.

In both cases, nonprofits played an important behind-the-scenes role. Nonprofits asked for the hearings, played a central part in developing witness lists, and took on the complicated task of coordinating the appearances of witnesses.

### Phone Calls

In just about every legislative campaign, there are times when it is crucial to have immediate contact from the grass roots. There is often less then twenty-four hours' notice before a key vote comes up in committee or even before a final vote in the legislature. Many nonprofits have a process for telephoning constituents at this critical point and urging calls to legislators. The fact that a legislator receives ten or twenty calls on your nonprofit's issue just before a vote can make a difference.

You can reach any member of Congress by calling (202) 224-3121. Using that number is almost as fast as calling the Congressperson's office directly. Telephone calls to district offices of legislators are second best. They achieve the objective of communicating your message, but there may be a crucial delay in a district office's reporting your call to the legislator, particularly if he or she is not in the district at the time.

When a vote is coming up, it may not be possible on short notice to talk by phone with your legislator, regardless of how well you know him or her. If you can't reach the legislator, ask for the legislative aide who is assigned to your issue. If you can't reach the aide, leave your message with the person who answered the phone. Legislative offices do keep count of the pro and con calls on issues, so at least be certain to leave your message. Keep your call brief. There will be little if any time to persuade. Your message can simply be two sentences, one asking for support and the other stating why. To help you make your point succinctly, you may want to write out your message and have it before you when you call.

If you want to get a last-minute message to the White House regarding your organization's views on a matter that the administration is considering, call the White House Comment Line at (202) 456-7639.

### Telegrams, Mailgrams, and Form Letters

Telegrams and mailgrams are less effective than personal letters or telephone calls, but they can help register last-minute opinions before a vote. It takes no more time, and perhaps less, to phone a legislator's office than to call in a telegram or a mailgram. Unless you have good reason not to, call the legislator directly instead of relying on a telegram or a mailgram. Form letters are better than nothing at all, but their volume must be huge to get attention.

## Other Communications

The number of ways you can use to get your story across to legislators is almost endless. Here are some examples:

1.  Invite your legislator to visit a facility that provides services to your clients, and describe how those services will be affected by his or her vote on your issue. Such a visit, which can be arranged for a time when the legislator will be in your district, is perhaps the most effective way of communicating a need.
2.  Have a legislator speak at a public meeting sponsored by your organization. Legislators usually appreciate such opportunities, if there is a chance to speak before a fairly large audience or if the audience is composed of people whom the legislator is particularly interested in reaching.
3.  Invite the legislator to meet your board of directors at the regular board meeting. You will probably know whether your legislator will want to want to attend. If you are uncertain, ask; there is nothing to lose.
4.  Some believe in holding receptions on Capitol Hill for legislators. These may provide opportunities to meet legislators or their staffs. In Washington, however, it is awfully difficult to turn out a large group of legislators on Capitol Hill. You often get very junior aides or interns, especially if it's late in the afternoon and there is food.
5.  Organize a Capitol Hill day, and invite members from throughout the area served by your group to participate. The arrangements are very time-consuming, and there is mixed opinion regarding this tactic's effectiveness. In my experience, however, this approach can be very helpful if participants are well briefed and if appointments with legislators are set up.
6.  Arrange for a number of two-person volunteer teams to visit legislators at the Capitol. If these key volunteers are leaders of your association, they may also profitably visit legislators from other districts. Appointments are always recommended but are critically important for people who are not constituents of legislators.
7.  A breakfast for legislators at a convenient location in the cap-

ital may be well attended because it does not cut into legislators' usual workday. Legislators are more likely to attend if they are invited by constituents who will also be there. Many state and local groups routinely use breakfasts as a forum for educating legislators.

When you find it expedient to do so, publicize any meetings that a legislator has with your organization.

# 6

# Maximizing Your Impact
# with Coalitions

Major legislation is enacted most often through the combined efforts of a number of groups working in coalition, rather than through the efforts of a single organization. With rare exceptions, only a coalition can produce contacts varied and influential enough to achieve success on a major public policy issue.

At their best, coalitions coordinate and focus the resources of many groups that have a common interest in a legislative issue. A coalition may be formed for an effort that will take only several months, or the effort may take years. It depends on the significance of the changes sought. While coalitions have the potential to garner enormous legislative strength, they remain fragile. They are always subject to the danger that some members will become dissatisfied with the direction being taken and will unilaterally attempt to arrange a legislative compromise not supported by the majority. Despite that inherent weakness, the risk is worth taking to gain the strength that comes from a broad base.

## Organizing a Coalition

There are a number of ways for you to determine whether there is interest among other groups in joining a coalition to work on a legislative issue. The simplest way is to describe, in a page or so, the problem as your organization sees it. Then invite groups to send representatives to a meeting. A person (perhaps yourself) whom all or most attendees know and respect should chair the first meeting. After several meetings, the group will probably want to select a permanent leader.

To avoid later misunderstandings, you should seek clear agreement from the outset on the goals of the coalition, how it will target its efforts, and how the undertaking will be financed. Financing is particularly important. If there is not clear agreement from the outset, the resulting dissension may undermine the coalition's effectiveness. As a coalition grows, a small "secretariat" is usually appointed. It is made up of the coalition's leaders and makes decisions that do not require the full coalition's approval.

The most important role of the secretariat is to build a sense of trust and openness, with honesty and "no surprises" paramount. Any compromises on legislation should be agreed to in advance by the coalition. The coalition may also give a small leadership group the power to make on-the-spot compromises. These are almost always required as legislation comes down to the finish line.

Every coalition must have one organization that serves as a clearinghouse. That organization attends, among other things, to all the exceedingly important mechanical details that go into the effective running of any meeting. (It is amazing how often such details, so important in making people feel at home, are neglected. A written agenda, name cards at each place, personal greetings by the host to each attendee, snacks—all these items help set the right tone for a meeting. Good attendance is aided if meetings are held at an established time and location and if coalition members are phoned in advance.) The clearinghouse organization also takes responsibility for receiving information from the coalition and, as necessary, passing that information on to coalition members, without delay. Because providing access to good, timely information is so important, the organization responsible for that function should be selected with great care.

Effective coalitions have leaders who recognize that the strength of the coalition, and therefore its ultimate success, rests with the coalition's members, not with its leaders. The leaders also recognize that their principal role is to serve the members by working hard at the unexciting but critically important details required for effective coordination with the clearinghouse organization.

## Working with a Coalition

There will be an inclination on the part of some coalition members to think the job is done once the coalition gets started: "The coalition will do it." It is very important to get the message across early that the success or failure of the coalition depends on the action of all its members. Get members involved immediately. Give them specific tasks, and hold them accountable by asking them to report regularly at coalition meetings.

It is wise to assess in advance the strength of the commitment of those being asked to join the coalition. It is essential that at least some coalition members view the coalition's issue as also the top priority for their own organizations. If no one organization sees the issue as paramount among its own concerns, it is almost impossible to generate the steam needed for a successful effort on a major legislative initiative. Passion will be lacking, and its absence always shows. The less passion there is, the more the coalition's effort will appear to legislators as simply another special-interest exercise, not as a reflection of constituents' real views. As a result, the coalition's effort will be largely discounted.

No coalition is ever fortunate enough to have its issue viewed as the top priority by the majority of its members. Moreover, the importance that individual coalition members assign to the issue often fluctuates during the life of the coalition, according to other legislative issues that the members may be addressing. Don't be disappointed if some members lose interest. That's in the nature of every coalition. Indeed, shifts in levels of enthusiasm provide a sense of renewal: those who show increasing interest can be given additional responsibility, while others, for good reasons that may have nothing to do with the coalition's efforts or leaders, will fall by the wayside. But if, over time, you find that many of your members are losing interest, it will be important for you to contact the groups that have dropped out recently and determine whether their interest has waned because of some failure on the part of the coalition's leaders.

The lobbying techniques that coalitions use are essentially the same as those that individual organizations use. Coalition members, like all members of organizations, need accurate, brief, clear, timely information on which to take action. Timeliness is sometimes especially difficult in coalition activity because there may be as many as four steps in the process of getting information to people who are asked to take action. It goes from the coalition to the national organization and then to the state group and the local association, which sends the information to its members. To speed up the process when a key vote is coming up in the near future, it is important for a coalition to consider using the telephone to get the word out quickly to its members. Nothing discourages a coalition member more than discovering that leaders were too late in getting them information on a crucial vote.

In making contacts with legislators, it is particularly helpful for coalition members to use the names of their individual organizations. Chances are that the legislator will be much more familiar with them than with the name of the coalition.

Legislation is one of the few areas of nonprofit organizational activity where there is a very clear outcome. Over time, you either succeed or fail in getting a measure enacted or voted down. Success in a legislative effort is almost like money in the bank for a nonprofit group. If publicized appropriately, a legislative success is very helpful in attracting volunteers and funding, and so there is always a temptation for the coalition's organizational leaders to claim credit for the victory. But this is shortsighted, if not unfair. The more you give coalition members credit for a victory and make them feel that they had an important role, the more they will want to participate in the continuing battle (if it's not over) or participate in any new efforts that the coalition may want to make. Spread the credit around as widely as possible, and you will strengthen all the members of the coalition. Stifle the inclination to do otherwise or to go quickly on to other things. Forget to give public acclaim to each coalition member, and you will miss an opportunity.

# 7

# Guidelines on Using a Government Relations Committee

The biggest mistake, bar none, made by government relations committees of nonprofits is to take on too many priorities. It is an understandable failing. In any nonprofit, so much needs to be done that volunteers as well as staff often cannot resist tackling yet another issue. As a result, the nonprofit often finds itself in the impossible situation of having several "number one" priority issues. Its efforts are spread so thin that nothing is done well.

A critically important rule that top volunteer and staff leaders must follow in any organization is to insist, painful though it may be, that the organization adopt only one top legislative priority. The committee can have twenty issues that it follows, but all must be ranked. There must be clear understanding that most of the issues will necessarily get only cursory attention.

Holding on to just one top priority is difficult. Committee members whose main interests are in different issues will push volunteers and staff people hard to give their issues top priority, even though the committee and the board have decided otherwise. Resist the temptation to give in. You may disappoint a key committee member, but you will serve your organization properly. Focusing on one issue at a time is the only way that you can marshal all your resources and ultimately prevail in the tough environment you face in any legislative fight. While keeping to one priority is important, there should also be enough flexibility in your process for the committee to shift emphasis to the second or third priority, if it becomes very clear that little more can be achieved for the moment on the legislation that is the top priority.

## How to Structure Your Government Relations Committee

A nonprofit's decisions on legislation are made by a variety of groups and individuals, but it is critically important to provide the means by which an established group has final authority to act when a legislative decision is needed immediately. That moment always comes, sooner or later, during the heat of a legislative campaign. When time doesn't permit consultation with the full government relations committee, two or three people should be given the authority to speak for the organization. That authority should be given on the basis of these people's judgment and their understanding of the positions already taken by the government relations committee, the board, and the full membership.

Because of the central role played by government relations activities in the overall programs of many nonprofits, most nonprofits give their committees policymaking rather than advisory status. Policymaking authority serves the useful function of permitting the committee to take positions and action on minor legislative issues without bringing them before the board. But be cautious. If the committee assumes too much authority, it may find itself without the power base to move a particular bill, because members may see the committee as having taken actions that the members did not really understand or support. Most nonprofits active in government relations give legislative activity a high priority. Therefore, it is important that the government relations committee, like the board of directors, be broadly representative of the organization's constituency.

Some committee members are valuable for their understanding of the legislative process; others, for their ability to chair subgroups of the committee; still others, for their contacts with influential members of the legislature. Some will be valuable because they understand the issues being addressed by the proposed legislation, even though they know little about the legislative process itself. The government relations committee sets the broad agenda, but much of the in-depth legislative work is delegated to task forces or other subgroups. These are usually headed by a government relations committee.

## Leading the Government Relations Committee

The most important attribute that the chair of your government relations committee can offer is his or her ability to lead. Expertise in the legislative process, although helpful, is not essential; other committee members and staff people have that knowledge. In nonprofits where government relations may be a key activity, it helps if the chair of the committee is a volunteer who both knows the organization well and has held key volunteer posts in the organization.

Being chair of the government relations committee gives the volunteer in that post very high visibility within the organization. Organzational leaders can provide that volunteer with an opportunity to strengthen his or her skills: serving as chair of this key committee often proves to be a stepping-stone to higher positions in the organization.

## Running the Committee Meeting

Nonprofits are noted for the number of meetings they hold. Strangely, however, their meetings are often not well conducted. There are ways to make a government relations committee meeting go smoothly. Staff members and the chair should meet well before the meeting, to determine what should be included in the meeting's agenda. Draw up an agenda packet, and include a cover note that states the main topics to be discussed. If the agenda packet also includes extensive readings, provide "executive summaries" (most committee members will not read lengthy materials). Mail the packet in time for members to receive it at least a week before the meeting. It also helps to provide brief biographical information on all committee members, including their addresses and telephone numbers. They may not know one another, and such a list will help them stay in touch.

At your last meeting of the year, set the meeting dates for the coming year. Send these dates to all committee members, and urge them to mark their calendars. A month before each meeting, send a reminder, along with an R.S.V.P. card. When in doubt, call several days before the meeting to confirm members' attendance.

Ask yourself what makes you feel at ease at a meeting. Greet each person at some point before the meeting begins. Provide extra agenda packets, and be certain to have a name card that stands upright (a "tent" card) at each person's place. (How often have you been embarrassed by having to hide the fact that you have forgotten the name of the person sitting across from you even though the two of you have met often in the past?) Unless you are very certain that everyone knows everyone else, have people introduce themselves. Go up to people who arrive late and greet them. Be certain that they have agenda packets and places at the table.

When more than one table is used, place the tables in a "square doughnut," so that all attendees will be facing the center and can all be heard easily. Check the room well before the meeting, to be certain that everything you have requested has been provided. Arrange for coffee and light snacks. You may be surprised how much they can help to set the right tone for your meeting.

This is sometimes very difficult, but don't let the chair, the staff, or any one person dominate the meeting. There is a strong temptation to stand aside when this happens. If you do, however, you stand to lose the interest, involvement, respect, and ultimately, the participation of the members. (For more information on these basic points, an excellent source is O'Connell, 1985; see especially the chapter called "Making the Most out of Meetings.")

# 8

# Lobbying
# Through the Media

Legislators, because of the important role the media play in shaping public opinion, pay special attention to issues covered by the media in their legislative districts. They also take note of the organizations and individuals the media quote in news stories on those issues.

Congressional staff people rank both news articles and editorials in major daily newspapers very high as forces that influence members of Congress (Burson-Marsteller, 1981). Articles and editorials in smaller publications rank a bit lower but still high. Effective media relations can be an important means of getting a legislator's support and influencing public opinion on your legislative issue.

There are a number of techniques for getting your message into the media—press releases, calling a reporter or editor, press conferences, letters to the editor, press interviews—but none is a sure thing! You can never be sure that your publicity efforts will produce so much as one spoken or written word on behalf of your cause, but it is important to try. (Sample press and media advisory notices are included in Resource D.)

There are some media activities that your organization can conduct without in-depth understanding of media relations. For example, you can probably get some letters to a newspaper editor

John Thomas, vice-president for communications at INDEPENDENT SECTOR wrote the final section of this chapter, "Special Opportunities with Radio and Television."

published by having key members of your board, or others with influence in the community, write to the editor. If you plan to develop a media strategy and become involved in press conferences, press interviews, press releases, meetings with editorial boards, and so on, then you should either enlist the services of a volunteer with public relations experience or hire a professional. A person with experience in media relations can save your group an enormous amount of effort by helping you know how and where to target your efforts most effectively.

If you plan to hire a consultant or staff member to conduct media relations, nothing can be more important than making the right decision and knowing the person's track record firsthand. Get an assessment from someone whose judgment you greatly respect, someone specifically acquainted with the person's or the public relations firm's work. Don't depend entirely on the general reputation of the individual firm, and don't rely wholly on how it describes its services. The closest to a foolproof approach in hiring the right person is to take an individual from a public relations firm or a consultant group who has worked either with your organization or with someone whose opinion you trust.

In dealings with the media, send them information only if it is truly newsworthy. You will be quickly and permanently dismissed if your so-called news is unimportant, inaccurate, or untimely.

There is a herd instinct in the media. If one influential newspaper picks up your story, others may quickly follow suit and contact you. If you can be responsive to all, your issue may maintain momentum for several days or even longer. Equally important, if the media have come to you as a source on this issue, they will view you as a source on related issues.

Reporters look for quotable sources, people they can count on for good one- or two-sentence comments that will add color and credibility to a story. It is wise to have that supposedly off-the-cuff comment well rehearsed before you talk with the reporter. It is also essential to be well briefed on an issue before giving an interview.

There should be close coordination between your organization's lobbyist and its media coordinator. The lobbyist can help with the media by being available for comment on pending legislation. The media coordinator must keep abreast of fast-breaking action on the legislation, to know when and how to get information and comments to the media.

Keep a list of media people who have contacted you or have written or spoken on your issue. They will be an important resource for future press conferences and press releases.

Your organization can present information to the media in a number of ways that will draw more attention to your issue and increase the interest of the legislature. The following sections discuss several media techniques often used by nonprofit groups.

### Press Releases

A press release can be used to make a statement or take a stand on actions by the legislature or the administration that affect your legislation. Whatever the subject of the press release, the information in it must be both important and new.

The release should be written concisely. The most important information should appear in the first paragraph, with the rest of the information given in descending order of importance. (Editors often cut paragraphs from the end of a story to fit it into the available space.)

The first page of a release should answer the "five w's"— *who, what, where, when,* and *why.* You will probably want to add *how* as well. Keep sentences and paragraphs brief. Use active rather than passive verbs, and hold the release to no more than a few pages. Accuracy in facts, spelling, and grammar are basic.

Type the release, double-spaced, on 8½" × 11" paper, and use wide margins. At the top of the page, state the name of the individual or group releasing the information, the name of the person in the organization whom the press should contact for more information, and a telephone number to call for more information. Include release instructions: "For immediate release, January 1989" or "For release at 1 P.M., January 10, 1991." Use quotations where appropriate, and clearly identify your sources.

### Press Conferences

It is usually difficult to get good attendance at press conferences, because there are always so many issues competing for the media's attention. If you are to have even moderate prospects for good attendance, your issue has to be particularly important and timely and your spokesperson well known.

Nothing can replace a skilled communications person in charge of making arrangements for a press conference. Whoever handles the conference should know the basics, including the hour of the day when reporters are most likely to attend, the location that will attract reporters, how far in advance the press must be notified and how best to do so, and which reporters are assigned to your issue. It is also important to give a reminder call on the day of the press conference. Have a well-written press statement and background materials available as handouts. Reporters often arrive, pick up those materials, and leave without waiting for the conference. Be certain that you have flawless audio equipment at the conference. Keep the press conference short, and leave time for a question-and-answer period. Always keep a list of those who have attended, for future follow-up.

### Letters to the Editor

Letters to the editor can increase awareness of your issue. Sometimes letters are used to respond to negative editorials or press stories (although some experts say that responding to a negative editorial through a letter to the editor only reinforces the negative points by repeating them in order to refute them).

If you think your legislation will be enhanced by letters to the editor, there are several points to keep in mind. Your letter should be tightly composed and should use short sentences. Check with the newspaper to determine the length of letters it prints. Use strong, active verbs. Avoid adjectives. Use specific examples to make your points. Address only one point per letter. Use accurate, up-to-date information. Don't attack the opposition. Always sign your name, and include your address and telephone number.

### Other Media Opportunities

Op-ed pieces, which appear opposite the newspaper's editorial page, provide an opportunity for individuals (usually well-known persons) to present in-depth views on various issues. Larger news-papers pay modest sums for op-ed pieces and assign editorial people to their op-ed pages.

Editorial boards of newspapers sometimes meet with well-known spokespersons from organizations that want to present their points of view on issues. With small and medium-sized newspapers, it is helpful to submit draft editorials. Small newspapers may print them word for word; bigger editorial staffs may find them useful in composing their own editorials. It's very important to thank repor-ters for their stories about your issue and to provide them with important new information that may constitute material for follow-up stories. Keep a file of reporters who have written on your issue.

## Special Opportunities With Radio and Television

Radio and television offer several kinds of opportunities for getting your message across. Some are specific to each medium and others are common to both. Radio and TV stations are accessible. Topics for talk shows, editorial themes, news stories—stations need all of these daily. Maybe you can help them fill their time and your needs.

The most obvious method is to get your story to the news departments of local radio and television stations. When circulating a news release to the print media, don't forget the news directors of radio and television stations. Most stations do have less time for news than newspapers have space, and so there is keen competition for stories, but keep trying. If you have a news-only station in your community, definitely go for it.

In the case of television news, it will help greatly if there is a visual angle to the story. If you can center the story on an inter-esting visual location, your chances are much better for making the TV news. Likewise, you may also want to consider a good visual location for a news conference—keeping in mind, of course, that news conferences should not be held unless you have real news to announce.

You can produce public service announcements for both radio and television, although some television spots are very expen-sive. Radio and television stations do offer public service time on a regular basis. The Federal Communications Commission no longer requires them to offer a specific amount of time, but most continue to provide some, to show that they are community-minded.

Your best chance of having both your radio and your TV public service spots used is to keep them short—about ten seconds for TV, and preferably nine. Perhaps you can supply one or two color slides to go with them. A television station may assist you in producing a video spot. It happens occasionally. It doesn't hurt to ask. But please understand if the station is too busy to do it.

Radio public service announcements can be longer—perhaps twenty or thirty seconds. Sometimes, however, just a sentence or two, targeted for use by a popular disc jockey several times during the day, can be very effective.

You can try to get your spokesperson on a radio or TV talk show. Perhaps your spokesperson can appear on a local call-in show. In either case, particularly the latter, be sure that the spokesperson is fully briefed on the issue and is prepared for criticism and strong comments from the opposite point of view.

You should not forget radio and television editorials. "What do you mean?" you may ask. "Radio and TV station managers write those, don't they?" Yes, they do. Most people don't realize, however, that many of those editorials are inspired and influenced by outside individuals and groups. Just as news tips come from outside in many cases, so do ideas for editorials. Again, it's not a sure thing, by any means. Station managers have to determine whether an issue is important to them and whether they agree with your side of the issue. But you can get in, and that chance is worth the effort to try.

# Part Two

# A GUIDE TO TECHNICAL ISSUES RELATED TO LOBBYING BY 501(c)(3) ORGANIZATIONS

The intent of Part Two is to provide enough information to volunteers and staff, especially to those who are new to lobbying, so that they will have a beginning understanding of it. This material should not replace legal counsel. If you have questions regarding any of the technical information, it will be important for you to consult with an attorney. Just remember that in the author's opinion, attorneys, with some notable exceptions, tend to be too cautious about encouraging nonprofits to lobby.

This book is about lobbying by nonprofits that are tax exempt under Section 501(c)(3) of the Internal Revenue Code. There are some limitations on the amount of lobbying a 501(c)(3) may conduct and those limitations are outlined in Chapter Nine.

One important difference between 501(c)(3) organizations and 501(c)(4)s is that charitable contributions are tax deductible to the former, but not to the latter. Additional information on lobbying by 501(c)(4) groups is provided in Chapter Ten.

# 9

# The 1976 Lobby Law
# and 1990 IRS Regulations:
# An Overview

In 1976, Congress passed landmark legislation that clarified and greatly expanded the extent to which nonprofits could lobby without jeopardizing their tax-exempt status. That legislation, Section 1307 of Public Law 94-455, recognized lobbying as an entirely proper function of nonprofits and ended the uncertainty about lobbying by groups that are tax-exempt under Section 501(c)(3) of the Internal Revenue Code.*

It took a full fourteen years for the Internal Revenue Service to issue final regulations under the 1976 lobby law, but the regulations were worth the wait. While the last four years included some stormy debate between nonprofits and the IRS regarding earlier proposed regulations, the final version, issued on August 31, 1990, is faithful to the 1976 law, which greatly extended the lobbying rights of nonprofits. There is clear consensus in the nonprofit community that the regulations provide a framework that will prove to be both flexible and workable for charities' efforts on legislation. In every critical area, the regulations reflect responsiveness to (although not complete acceptance of) the criticisms and suggestions

---

*Public Law 94-455 resulted in Internal Revenue Code Sections 4911 and 501(h). Section 4911 includes information on how much can be spent on lobbying. Section 501(h) provides information on electing to come under the provisions of PL 94-455.

offered by nonprofits during the long process that led to the final outcome.

In understanding the 1976 lobby law, it helps to know that lobbying, for a nonprofit electing to come under the law, is only the expenditure of money by the organization for the purpose of attempting to influence legislation. Where there is no expenditure by the organization for lobbying, there is no lobbying by the organization. Therefore, lobbying by a volunteer for a nonprofit is not counted as a lobbying expenditure to the organization and is *not* lobbying. If, however, the volunteer is reimbursed by the nonprofit for out-of-pocket expenditures, then the reimbursed funds do count as a lobbying expenditure. But it's important to keep in mind the point that *lobbying occurs only when there is an expenditure of funds* for an activity that meets the other criteria for lobbying.

It is also helpful in understanding the 1976 law to recognize that the law defines two kinds of lobbying: direct lobbying and grass-roots lobbying. To oversimpify, the term *direct lobbying* means communications that your organization has about legislation (1) with legislators or government officials who participate in the formulation of legislation and (2) with its own members. Direct lobbying would include visiting a congressperson about a bill and being in touch with your organization's members and urging them to contact legislators. The term *grass-roots lobbying* refers to any attempt to influence legislation through an attempt to affect the opinion of the general public. The ceiling for a nonprofit's spending on grass-roots lobbying is one-fourth of the total allowable lobbying expenditures.

Sometimes groups confuse urging their members to lobby with grass-roots lobbying of the general public. They mistakenly think that contacting their members, who may number hundreds of thousands, to urge them in turn to contact members of the legislature constitutes grass-roots lobbying, simply because those members are at the grass-roots level. Only when an organization is trying to reach beyond its members to get action from the general public does grass-roots lobbying occur.

The following information on the 1976 law is fairly detailed, but don't be discouraged by all the detail. Keep in mind that the provisions of the law are very generous. They provide all the lobbying latitude that ninety-nine out of one-hundred groups will ever need. The details included here will help provide the assurance you may need that many of your activities in the legislative arena are not lobbying under the 1976 lobby law.

Virtually all of the information that follows in this chapter is drawn from materials written for INDEPENDENT SECTOR by Walter B. Slocombe of Caplin & Drysdale, Washington, D.C. It is an overview of the lobbying latitude permitted to 501(c)(3) organizations under the 1976 law and regulations.

## Public Charity Lobbying: An Overview

### *What Groups Are Affected?*

The regulations are effective for an organization's first tax year that begins after their publication, which took place on August 31, 1990. Public charities that have elected to come under the 1976 lobby law need to familiarize themselves with the regulations, so that they will know what activities will and will not count against the statutory limits, and so that they can correctly calculate the amounts they treat as spending for lobbying.

Private foundations are affected. This is because the regulations (1) elaborate the standards that foundations must meet to comply with the general ban on lobbying by private foundations and (2) establish guidelines for grants by private foundations to public charities that elect to come under the law.

Public charities that have any degree of involvement in public policy issues also have an interest in the regulations, even if they have not elected to be covered by them. This interest arises partly because public charities need to decide whether to make that election, now that its effects are clearer, and partly because, although the regulations nominally apply to public charities only if they have so elected, the standards set forth in the regulations may affect the application of the old "substantiality" standard, to which non-electing charities will remain subject.

### *How Does the Tax Law Regulate Public Charities' Lobbying?*

The general rule of Section 501(c)(3), to which all organizations exempt under that provision are subject unless they elect to come

under the 1976 lobby law is that "no substantial part" of their activities may be that of attempting to influence legislation. Although
the provision has been in the IRS code since 1934 and has occasionally been applied by the courts, there has never been a clear definition of the point at which lobbying becomes substantial or, indeed,
of what activities related to public policy and to controversial subjects constitute attempts to influence legislation. In particular, the
IRS position is that spending, as a share of budget, is far from the
sole measure of whether a nonelecting group's lobbying is substantial; such factors as absolute amount spent, impact, public promi-
nence, and unpaid volunteer work also enter into the determination.

   To clarify and liberalize the rules for lobbying by charities,
Sections 501(h) and 4911 were added to the code in 1976, as a result
of the enactment of the 1976 lobby law. In outline, the provisions
permit most public charities (but not churches, their integrated aux-
illiaries, or a convention or association of churches) to elect to have
their legislative efforts governed by the specific rules of Sections
501(h) and 4911, instead of the vague "substantiality" standard. To
that end, the 1976 legislation both sets financial limits for lobbying
activities and defines the activities that count against those limits.

### What Are the Main Elements of the 1976 Law?

*Exclusions from Lobbying.* Critical to the 1976 law are the provisions declaring that many expenditures that have some relationship
to public policy and legislative issues are not treated as lobbying
and so are permitted without limit. These include expenditures for
the following:

1.  Communications to members of an organization that discuss
    legislation but do not urge action by the members
2.  Making available the results of a "nonpartisan analysis, study
    or research" on a legislative issue that presents a sufficiently
    full and fair exposition of the pertinent facts to enable the
    audience to form an independent opinion
    (The regulations make clear that research and analysis need not
    be "neutral" or "objective" to fall within this "nonpartisan"
    exclusion. The exclusion is available to research and analysis

that take direct positions on the merits of legislation, as long as the organization presents facts fully and fairly, makes the material generally available, and does not include a direct call to the reader to contact legislators.)

3. Responding to written requests from a legislative body (not just a single legislator) for technical advice on pending legislation

4. So-called self-defense activity—that is, lobbying legislators (but not the general public) on matters that may affect the organization's own existence, powers, exempt status, and similar matters

   (Lobbying for programs in the organization's field, however, is not self-defense lobbying.)

5. Discussion of broad social, economic, and similar policy issues whose resolution would require legislation, as long as there is no discussion of specific legislative measures.

*Permitted Levels of Spending for Lobbying.* The second key element of the 1976 law is that it unequivocally declares that activities that do constitute active lobbying are permitted, provided only that they fall within the spending ceilings established by the law. The spending ceilings are based on percentages of the charity's budget for the year, beginning at 20 percent of the first $500,000 and ending at 5 percent of expenditures over $1.5 million. (Strictly speaking, the base is the charity's exempt-purpose expenditures, which include all payments for the organization's programs and exempt purposes but exclude costs of investment management, unrelated businesses, and certain fund-raising costs.) There is an overall maximum ceiling of $1 million a year. The effect of the sliding-scale ceilings is that an organization reaches the maximum permissible ceiling when its exempt-purpose expenditures reach $17 million.

Expenditures for grass-roots lobbying—that is, attempting "to influence legislation through an attempt to affect the opinions of the general public or any segment thereof"—are limited to one-quarter of the overall ceiling, as already stated. Amounts spent on lobbying in excess of that level must be for direct lobbying—that is, for communications made directly to legislators and their staffs and to executive-branch officials who participate in the formulation of legislation. (As previously described, communications with an organization's members that urge them to contact legislators are also treated as direct, rather than grass-roots, lobbying. The total and grass-roots ceilings at various exempt-purpose expenditure levels are shown in Table 4.) Since the amount that may be spent on grass-roots lobbying is limited to one-quarter of the overall lobbying limit, if an organization's total lobbying limit is $100,000, then it may spend the full $100,000 on direct lobbying or it may spend up to $25,000 on grass-roots lobbying and the rest on direct lobbying. Even if it chooses to spend nothing on direct lobbying, it will still be limited to $25,000 on grass-roots lobbying.

*Flexible Sanctions.* A third important element of the 1976 legislation was the establishment of a new and more flexible system of sanctions, to replace the "death sentence" of loss of exemption as the principal sanction for violation of the "substantiality" standard. (Since 1976, Congress has added additional sanctions, beyond loss of exemption, for non-electing organizations that violate that standard—a 5 percent excise tax on excessive lobbying spending, and a similar tax on managers who willfully and unreasonably agree to lobbying expenditures, knowing that these are likely to cause loss of exemption.) The initial sanction for public charities under the 1976 law that spend more than either the overall or the grass-roots limit is a 25 percent excise tax on the lobbying spending in any year in excess of the ceiling. (If both ceilings are exceeded, the tax is on the greater of the two excess amounts.) Loss of exemption is an available sanction only if spending normally exceeds 150 percent of either the overall or the grass-roots limit, generally determined by aggregating both spending and limits over a four-year period.

### What Spending Counts Against the Limits?

There is considerable uncertainty about what activity counts against the "substantiality" standard, but the standard, under the 1976 lobby law, is strictly financial. The only factor that must be taken into account is the cost of communications for direct or grass-roots lobbying, including the cost of preparing the communication (such as staff time, facilities, and allocable overhead).

Table 4. Lobbying Ceilings under the 1976 Lobby Law.

| Exempt-Purpose Expenditures | Total Lobbying Expenditures | Amount of Total Allowable for Grass-roots Lobbying |
|---|---|---|
| Up to $500,000 | 20% of exempt-purpose expenditures | One-quarter |
| $500,000–$1 million | $100,000 +15% of excess over $500,000 | $25,000 + 3.75% of excess over $500,000 |
| $1 million–$1.5 million | $175,000 + 10% of excess over $1 million | $43,750 + 2.5% of excess over $1 million |
| $1.5 million–$17 million | $225,000 + 5% of excess over $1.5 million | $56,250 + 1.25% of $1.7 excess over $1.5 million |
| Over $17 million | $1 million | $250,000 |

*Elements Required for a Lobbying Communication.* To be a direct lobbying communication, and therefore to count against the direct lobbying limits, a communication must refer to specific legislation and reflect a point of view on its merits. "Specific legislation" includes a specific measure that has not yet been introduced but does not include general concepts for solving problems that have not yet been reduced to legislative proposals.

To be a grass-roots lobbying communication, subject to the lower ceiling, in most cases, a communication must, apart from referring to specific legislation and reflecting a view on it, encourage recipients to contact legislators. Under the regulations, such a call to action exists only when the material directly tells its audience to contact legislators; provides a legislator's address, phone number, or similar information; provides a petition, postcard, or other prepared message to be sent to the legislator; or identifies one or more legislators as opposing the organization's views, being undecided, being recipients' representative(s), or being a member of the committee that will consider the legislation.

Under these rules, a public charity (except in the narrow case of "highly publicized legislation," to be discussed) can make any public statement it likes about a legislative issue, without having the costs counted against its grass-roots lobbying limit—as long as it avoids calls to action. The broad freedom that this rule gives charities to discuss issues freely, as long as they forgo calls to action, is shown by an example in the regulations. It concerns a mass-media advertisement that the IRS says would not normally be considered grass-roots lobbying, because it lacks such a call. The sample advertisement reads as follows: "The State Assembly is considering a bill to make gun ownership illegal. This outrageous legislation would violate your constitutional rights and the rights of other law-abiding citizens. If this legislation is passed, you and your family will be criminals if you want to exercise your right to protect yourselves."

*Special Rule for Paid Mass-Media Messages Close to Votes on "Famous" Bills.* There is one exception to the rule stating that a public communication about legislation must include a call to action in order to be considered lobbying. The regulations eliminate the "call to action" requirement in a narrowly defined set of cases involving mass-media advertising just before a vote on certain legislation that has elicited a high degree of public awareness. These regulations apply—and communications can be considered grass-roots lobbying, even without a call to the public to communicate with legislators about the legislation—only when all the following conditions are met:

1. The legislation in question has received so much publicity that its pendency or its general terms, purpose, or effect are known to a significant element of the general public, not just to the particular interest groups directly affected. The degree of publicity given the legislation is a factor here, but there must not only be publicity; there must also be general public knowledge about the particular legislation.
2. The public charity has bought paid advertising in the mass media (meaning television, radio, billboards, or general-circulation newspapers and magazines). Direct mail and the organization's own media outlets are not considered paid media, except for radio and television broadcasting by the organization itself and organization-published periodicals that have a circulation of 100,000, more than half of which is outside the organization's membership.

3.   The advertising appears within two weeks before a vote will be taken in a full house or full committee (not just a subcommittee).
4.   The advertisement either
     a.   refers directly to the legislation (as in the gun control ad above) but does not include a call to action, as defined under the general standards,* or
     b.   states a view on the general subject of the legislation and urges the public to communicate with legislators about that subject. (To carry on the handgun example, such an ad might say, "Let your state assemblyman know you want to protect your right to keep and bear arms"—without referring directly to the pending bill.)

Even when all these conditions are present, the organization can avoid counting the ad as a lobbying cost if it can show that it has customarily run such ads without regard to the timing of legislation, or that the particular ad's timing was unrelated to the upcoming legislative action (as may be the case when television ads are bought under conditions that allow the station to determine when they run). This special rule for ads on highly publicized and well-known legislation affect few if any activities that are not directly and consciously aimed at legislative results. Even in those cases, of course, the activity is permitted within financial ceilings.

*Special Rule for Referenda, Initiatives, and Similar Procedures.* In general, legislative messages aimed at the public as a whole are grass-roots lobbying if they meet the "call to action" standard. The final regulations, however, recognize that in the case of referenda, initiatives, and similar procedures, the public is itself the legislature. Accordingly, communications to the public that refer to such measures and that take a stand on them are treated as direct lobbying of a legislature—subject only to the higher ceiling. The effect of these rules is that communications (newspaper ads, for example) that refer to a ballot measure and reflect a view on it are direct lobbying, whether or not they explicitly tell people how to vote.

*If the ad includes a call to action, it is grass-roots lobbying without the special "mass media" rules.

This rule gives public charities important flexibility to be active in referendum efforts, which would have been impractical if they had been forced to count against the lower grass-roots lobbying limits.

### When Does Later Use of Materials in Lobbying Cause Their Costs to Be Counted as Lobbying?

The costs of a lobbying communication include the costs of the staff and facilities needed to prepare it, not just the costs of paper and ink or videotape. An issue of concern to many groups, especially those doing research on public policy issues, has been the possibility that research costs might be treated as costs of preparing to lobby, if the published results of the research were later referred to and used in lobbying. The final regulations on this so-called "subsequent use" issue should greatly ease organizations' concerns that their lobbying spending will be boosted unexpectedly because materials they have prepared are later used in lobbying—whether the use is by the organization itself, by a related organization, or by a third party. This is because costs of materials that are not themselves used for lobbying need to be counted as lobbying-support costs (on the basis of their later use in lobbying) *only* in cases in which all of the following conditions exist:

1.  The materials both refer to and reflect a view on specific legislation. (They do not, however, in their initial format, include a call to action. If the materials do include such a call, their public circulation would itself be grass-roots lobbying.) Materials—such as raw research data—that do not meet this test are entirely outside the "subsequent use" rules.
2.  The lobbying use occurs within six months of payment for the materials. Therefore, lobbying use more than six months after a research project is complete cannot affect the organization's lobbying costs. In any case, only the most recent six months of spending potentially represents a lobbying cost. There is no risk that, because of some lobbying use of research results more than six months after a project is finished, years of accumulated research spending will be treated as lobbying costs.
3.  The organization fails to make a substantial nonlobbying dis-

tribution of the materials before the lobbying use. If the materials are "nonpartisan, analysis, study, or research," a nonlobbying distribution qualifies as "substantial" (and therefore excludes all the costs from lobbying treatment) if it conforms to the normal distribution pattern for similar materials, as followed by that organization and similar ones. For other materials, the nonlobbying distribution must be at least as extensive as the lobbying distribution. This rule means that, by seeing that research-and-analysis materials that take positions on legislation are first distributed to the public in normal ways, an organization can prevent their costs from being treated as lobbying costs, even if the materials are later used in lobbying by the organization itself or by an affiliate.

4.  The organization's primary purpose in creating the materials was to use them in lobbying rather than for some nonlobbying goal. When the lobbying use is by an unrelated organization, not only must there be clear and convincing evidence of such a lobbying purpose but that evidence must also include evidence of collusion and cooperation with the organization using the material for lobbying.

For private foundations making grants to public charities that spend the money on materials later used in lobbying, there is another layer of protection. Even if the grantee violates the "subsequent use" rules, the grantor foundation can be taxed on the grant as a lobbying expenditure only if the private foundation had a primary lobbying purpose in making the grant or if the grantmaking foundation knew or should reasonably have known of the grantee's lobbying purpose.

The cumulative effect of these safeguards is that a research organization can readily avoid any risk of unexpected lobbying expenses. Only costs that are less than six months old can be at issue. Even in theory, the problem can arise only in the case of material that takes a position on specific legislation. Even for such materials, there is a safe harbor for distributions that follow the normal patterns of dissemination. In any event, an organization can avoid having costs for materials later used in lobbying treated as grassroots lobbying cost if the primary purpose of incurring the cost was

a nonlobbying objective. If the later use is by an unrelated organization, there must be clear and convincing evidence that the organization developed the research for the purpose of lobbying.

### Does Electing to Be Governed by the New Regulations Complicate Receiving Grants from Foundations?

Private foundations may not elect to come under the 1976 law, and
they remain absolutely prohibited from making expenditures for
lobbying purposes. Therefore, some foundations have been concerned about their ability to make grants to nonprofits that explicitly adopt programs of lobbying by electing to come under the 1976
lobby law, and some nonprofits have worried that making an election under the 1976 law will scare off foundation funders.

The regulations—codifying and even liberalizing long-estab-
lished IRS policy—meet these concerns by setting up a highly protective system for grants by private foundations to public charities
that elect to come under the 1976 law. Under these rules, a foundation may make without tax liability a general-purpose grant to a
public charity that lobbies, whether or not the public charity has
elected. A private foundation may also make a grant to support a
specific project that includes lobbying, as long as its own grant is
less than the amount budgeted for the nonlobbying parts of the
project. For example, if a specific project has a $200,000 budget, of
which $20,000 is to be spent for lobbying, a private foundation can
give the project up to $180,000 because that is the part of the project
budget allocated to nonlobbying uses. The fact that other private
foundations have already made grants for the project need not be
taken into account in considering how much a private foundation
can give. Of course, the foundation cannot earmark its funds for
lobbying, nor can a foundation support research in a case where the
foundation itself has a primary lobbying purpose and where the
results are used in violation of the "subsequent use" rules.

The regulations make clear that a foundation can rely on
statements by the prospective grantee regarding how much the project will spend on lobbying, unless the foundation knows or has
reason to know that the statements are false. The regulations also
make clear that as long as the granting foundation complies with

these standards when it makes the grant, it will not be held to have made a taxable lobbying expenditure if the public charity violates the assurances it gave when seeking the grant.

### When Will a Public Charity's Transfers to a Lobbying Organization Be Counted as Lobbying Expenditures?

If a public charity pays another organization or an individual to do lobbying for it, the payment counts against its direct or grass-roots lobbying ceiling according to the character of the work done. The regulations also seek to prevent evasion of the limits by public charities that provide funds to other organizations not subject to the Section 501(c)(3) lobbying limits—such as presumably a related organization exempt under Section 501(c)(4)—to increase the resources available for the recipient's lobbying efforts. In such a case, the funds transferred are deemed to have been paid for grass-roots lobbying, to the extent of the transferee's grass-roots lobbying expenditures, with any remaining amount treated as having been paid for direct lobbying, to the extent of the transferee's direct lobbying expenditures.

This rule is subject to some very important qualifications, however. There is no lobbying expenditure when a public charity makes a grant to a noncharity and the grant's use is expressly limited to a specific educational or otherwise charitable purpose and when records demonstrate that use. The regulations also make clear that the rule does not apply when the public charity is getting fair market value for the money it transfers. Thus, if a 501(c)(3) organization pays rent at fair market value to a 501(c)(4) group, or if the 501(c)(3) group pays to a 501(c)(4) group its proper portion of the costs of a shared employee, the rule does not apply, because the 501(c)(3) group is getting full value from the 501(c)(4) group.

These transfer rules protect public charities that engage in normal and legitimate transactions with related (or unrelated) entities. Such charities need only follow the substantive and accounting procedures that are required in any case for general tax purposes, without regard to the special lobbying provisions.

*What Accounting Is Required for Lobbying Expenditures?*

All Section 501(c)(3) organizations—whether or not they elect to
come under the 1976 lobby law—must report on their annual IRS
Form 990 the total amount of their lobbying expenditures. The only
additional requirement for electing organizations is that they must
break the expenditures down by direct and grass-roots activities.
Both classes of organizations must maintain records to support the
entries on the return—showing, for example, the basis for comput-
ing the overhead allocated to lobbying activities.

*How Are Expenditures That Have Both Lobbying and
Nonlobbying Purposes Treated?*

Sometimes a public charity wants to distribute a communication
that has both lobbying and nonlobbying messages, such as a mass
mailing that calls for readers to contact legislators about pending
legislation and also asks them for contributions to the organization.
In general, the regulations permit allocation between the lobbying
and nonlobbying aspects of such mixed-purpose communications;
but, to reflect the special solicitude that is extended to communications with members, treatment of such communications is more
generous.

The details are beyond the scope of this overview, but the
general situation is as follows. First, costs of communications with
members may be allocated, as between lobbying and any other bona
fide nonlobbying purpose (education, fund raising, or advocacy on
nonlegislative issues), on any reasonable basis. An attempt to allocate to lobbying only the particular words actually urging legislative action—and not the material explaining the legislative issue
and the organization's position—will be rejected as unreasonable.
Second, costs for part-lobbying communications to nonmembers
(including even the membership share, if the communications go
primarily to nonmembers) can be allocated to nonlobbying purposes only to the extent they do not address the "same specific
subject" as the legislative message in the communication. The
"same specific subject" is rather broadly defined to include activities
that would be affected by legislation addressed elsewhere in the

message, as well as the background and consequences of the legislation and activities affected by it. Nevertheless, fund raising and providing general information about the organization are not treated as being on the "same specific subject" as a legislative message. Therefore, that share of costs attributable to those goals would not be a lobbying expenditure. Allocation of costs away from lobbying is also permitted for the parts of a communication that are discussions of distinct aspects of a broad problem, one feature of which would be affected by the legislation addressed elsewhere in the communication.

Organizations that have extensive and expensive direct-mail operations aimed at current contributors (who are members) and prospects (who are not) will need to review their mailings, to ensure that they do not inadvertently make large grass-roots lobbying expenditures. Similarly, groups that routinely send legislative alerts to nonmembers may want to make them distinct publications, rather than combining them with general communications.

### When Are Several Nonprofits Treated on an Aggregate Basis?

In general, ceiling determinations and lobbying expenditure calculations are made on a separate basis for each legally distinct 501(c)(3) organization. Only if two or more organizations are subject to common control through interlocking majorities on their boards (or to common control by a third organization), or if one organization is required by its governing instrument to follow the legislative decisions of another, are the organizations aggregated under a single ceiling, with aggregate computations of expenditures. The requirement to follow legislative decisions must be express and not merely implied.

### For Further Information

The preceding analysis is intended to give interested volunteers and staff members an overview, in lay language, of the 1976 lobby law. No guide, however, can adequately substitute for official information. Those wishing to make their own analyses will find the following additional sources to be of value:

- U.S. Internal Revenue Code of 1986, as amended, especially Sections 501(a), 501(c)(3), 501(h), and 4911.
- Public Law no. 94-455, The Tax Reform Act of 1976, approved October 4, 1976 (specifically, Section 1307, "Lobbying by Public Charities").
- House Report no. 94-1210, "Influencing Legislation by Public Charities," June 2, 1976, to accompany H.R. 13500. (H.R. 13500 became Section 1307 of PL 94-455.)
- Senate Report no. 94-938, Part 2, supplemental report on additional amendment to H.R. 10612, July 20, 1976. (H.R. 10612 became PL 94-455.)
- House Report no. 94-1515, conference report on H.R. 10612, September 13, 1976.
- "Final Regulations on Lobbying by Public Charities and Private Foundations." *Federal Register,* Aug. 31, 1990, p. 35579.

### Election Procedure for Nonprofits

The process for electing to come under the 1976 lobby law (PL 94-455) is very simple, which no doubt partly accounts for the fact that more than three thousand nonprofits, large and small, have chosen to do so since 1976. Those eligible to so elect are nonprofits exempt from taxation by Section 501(c)(3) of the Internal Revenue Code. The legislation does not apply to churches, their integrated auxiliaries, or a convention or association of churches. Private foundations also are not eligible, although they may make grants to nonprofits that do elect.

If a nonprofit does not elect to take advantage of the generous lobbying provisions under the 1976 lobby law, it remains subject to the vague "insubstantial" rule that has been in the tax code since 1934. Under that provision, if a charity engages in more than "insubstantial" lobbying, it loses its Section 501(c)(3) status and its right to receive tax-deductible charitable contributions. Unfortunately, "insubstantial" has never been defined under the law, with the result that nonprofits that do lobby but have not elected to come under the 1976 law cannot be certain how much lobbying they may conduct without jeopardizing their tax-exempt status. Many nonprofits have followed the questionable guideline that the expenditure of 5 percent of their total annual expenditures on lobbying is not substantial and is therefore within the law. They have assumed that 5 percent of their *expenditures* is permissible because of a 1955 Sixth Circuit Court of Appeals ruling to the effect that attempts to influence legislation that constitute 5 percent of total *activities* are not substantial.

There is good reason to doubt that the "5 percent test" should be relied on. It was called into question by a 1972 ruling, which rejected a percentage test in determining what constituted substantial lobbying. In that case, the Tenth Circuit Court of Appeals supported a "facts and circumstances" test instead of a percentage test. In a 1974 ruling, the Claims Court stated that a percentage test was deemed inappropriate for determining whether lobbying activities are substantial. It was found that an exempt organization enjoying considerable prestige and influence could be considered as having a substantial impact on the legislative process, solely on the basis of making a single official position statement—an activity that would be considered negligible if measured according to a percentage standard of time expended. It is clearly in the interest of every nonprofit that lobbies more than a nominal amount to consider electing to come under the provisions of the 1976 law.

The law makes the process for electing very easy. A nonprofit's governing body—that is, its executive committee, board of directors, other representatives, or total membership, according to the constitution or bylaws of the particular nonprofit—may elect to have the organization come under the law. An authorized officer or trustee signs the one-page Internal Revenue Service Form 5768 and checks the box marked "Election." (A copy of IRS Form 5768 is in Resource E.) Regardless of the actual date of election, the nonprofit is considered to have come under the provisions of the law as of the start of the tax year during which it files the election.

The nonprofit automatically continues under the provisions of the 1976 law unless it chooses to revoke that election. It can do that by having its governing body vote on revocation and having an authorized officer or trustee sign another Form 5768. The revocation becomes effective at the start of the tax year that follows the date of the revocation. In other words, revocation can only be prospective.

A new nonprofit may elect to come under the lobby law even before it is determined to be eligible by the IRS. It simply submits Form 5768 at the time it submits its "Application for Recognition of Exemption" (Form 1023). Offices and addresses for obtaining IRS Form 5768 are listed in Resource F. The nonprofit's employer identification number, which is requested at the top of the form, is listed on the nonprofit's "Employer Quarterly Federal Tax Return" (Form 941).

One final important note: some nonprofits have been reluctant to come under the 1976 lobby law, for fear that taking this action will serve as a "red flag" to the IRS and prompt an audit of lobbying activities. Fortunately, this is not the case. The Internal Revenue Service, in an October 7, 1988, letter to attorneys representing INDEPENDENT SECTOR, made clear that it does not plan to single out nonprofit organizations that elect to come under the provisions of the 1976 law. (Earlier, the Internal Revenue Service had furnished each IRS region with a listing of organizations that had elected to come under the 1976 law, and that action had raised fears among some nonprofits that the IRS planned to target for audit the lobbying activities of those nonprofits that had elected.) In the letter, the IRS representative said, "As I stated above, our intent has been, and continues to be, one of encouragement [of nonprofit organizations] to make the election. Accordingly, I am taking steps to see that the IR Manual provision on this is revised. I have instructed that the IR Manual clarify that the filing of an election is a neutral factor for audit selection purposes. This change should eliminate the perception and concerns expressed in your letter." In compliance with that promise, the Internal Revenue Manual now states, "Experience also suggests that organizations that have made the election [under the 1976 lobby law] are usually in compliance with the restrictions on legislative activities, so they do not appear to justify an effort to examine solely on this issue."

When Congress was debating the 1976 lobby law, before its enactment, there was clear evidence that Congress fully intended the law to encourage nonprofits to lobby and not to discourage them by singling them out for audit. These facts should reassure nonprofit groups that they will not be targeted for lobbying audits if they elect to be covered under the 1976 law.

# 10

# Special Issues
# and Regulations

### Lobbying by Nonprofits on Initiatives and Referenda

An initiative is a procedure by which a specified number of voters propose a statute, constitutional amendment, or ordinance and compel a popular vote on its adoption. One good example of nonprofits' effective use of the initiative process to achieve their program goals is the continuing successful efforts of state and local affiliates of the American Cancer Society, the American Heart Association, and the American Lung Association. Working in coalition, they have had the banning of smoking in public facilities put to a vote in a number of states and communities.

Sometimes called "do-it-yourself government" because they bypass legislative bodies, initiatives cover a wide variety of issues: a nuclear-arms freeze, tax cuts, reduced state spending, deposits on soft-drink bottles, civilians' use of nuclear power to generate electricity, greater citizen control over state supervision or regulation of electric utilities, prohibitions on abortion funding for low-income women, changing the way state or local legislatures are redistricted, and changes in state laws dealing with crime. The initiative involves getting the number of signatures of bona fide voters required by the state constitution or local charter to sign petitions mandating the legislature to place the issue on the ballot. It is expensive and cumbersome to get an initiative all the way through to the ballot, and chances are only four in ten that the initiative will be approved. Nevertheless, the popularity of initiatives has grown dramatically in the past ten years.

A referendum is a procedure for referring or submitting measures already passed by a legislative body to the electorate, for approval or rejection. Bond issues for new schools, highways, and pollution control are typical examples of measures passed by local government and then placed before the general electorate for final action.

Under the 1976 lobby law, IRS regulations recognize that in referenda, initiatives, and similar procedures, the public itself is the legislature. Therefore, communications to the public that refer to an initiative or referendum are treated as direct lobbying, not grass-roots lobbying. Nonprofits' ceiling for spending on direct lobbying is four times as much as the ceiling on grass-roots lobbying. It follows that nonprofits have more latitude to lobby on behalf of an initiative or a referendum than they would have had if (as some had feared) the final IRS regulations had said that such lobbying is grass-roots lobbying. This means that a nonprofit—in a newspaper ad, for example—can refer to a specific initiative or referendum, reflect a view on the proposal, and urge readers not only to vote for or against the initiative or referendum but also to ask their neighbors to do likewise. The nonprofit can then charge all of it as direct lobbying. (Under IRS regulations, such activities aimed at the general public on legislation other than initiatives, referenda, and similar procedures are considered grass-roots lobbying and are therefore subject to the lower expenditure limit.)

It is clear that initiatives, referenda, and similar processes provide an opportunity for nonprofit lobbying that has been largely overlooked until recently. All states have provisions of some kind permitting citizens to vote directly on legislation. The liberal IRS rules regarding nonprofit lobbying on initiatives and referenda should provide enormously increased incentives for nonprofits to enter into this arena.

### Voter Education by Nonprofits During a Political Campaign

Nonprofits sometimes confuse working for the election of a political candidate with lobbying. These two kinds of activity are in fact very different. It is perfectly legal (and highly appropriate) for a nonprofit to work for the passage of a particular piece of legislation, during a political campaign or at any other time. Working for the election of a particular political candidate, however, federal, state, or local—is strictly prohibited and is cause for the nonprofit to lose its tax-exempt status.

In the past, there was considerable uncertainty about the voter-education activities that nonprofits could conduct during a political campaign without jeopardizing their tax-exempt status. That uncertainty had grown out of 1954 legislation by Congress to the effect that a 501(c)(3) organization must "not participate in, or intervene in (including publishing or distributing statements), any political campaign on behalf of any candidate for public office." The problem for nonprofits was that Congress had not clarified this language, and the IRS had published no regulations. To clarify the latitude available to nonprofits to carry out voter-education activities, INDEPENDENT SECTOR sought letter rulings by the IRS. Letter rulings state how the IRS applies the tax law and regulations to particular circumstances. Although they formally bind the IRS only in the case of the individual organization that receives the letter ruling, they do provide guidance on IRS thinking about similar situations with other organizations. Two rulings received in 1980 have provided extremely important guidance.

While a 501(c)(3) group cannot work on behalf of or against candidates, the IRS letter rulings to INDEPENDENT SECTOR indicate that there are a number of other voter activities that it can legally engage in.

### Electioneering

A 501(c)(3) organization cannot endorse, contribute to, work for, or otherwise support a candidate for public office, nor can it oppose one. This in no way prohibits officers, individual members, or employees from participating, provided that they say or do everything as private citizens and not as spokespersons for the organization or while using the organization's resources. If they choose to identify themselves with the organization, they must make it plain that they are speaking solely for themselves and not for the organization. If members do not identify themselves with the organization but the media do, the members have done nothing wrong.

### Candidates' Statements

It is entirely proper for a nonprofit to inform candidates of its positions on particular issues and to urge them to go on record, pledging their support of those positions. Such action from candidates is often very helpful in getting legislation enacted that is favored by nonprofits. Such statements become useful to nonprofits after an election is over. For example, before the election of 1980, in a communication to Catholic Charities USA, Republican presidential candidate Ronald Reagan endorsed the charitable deduction for nonitemizers. That statement was later used, repeatedly and effectively, with members of Congress and the administration to develop support for the provision.

Candidates may distribute their responses both to the nonprofit and to the general public. Nonprofits, however, do not have the same freedom. They may not publish or distribute statements by candidates except as nonpartisan "questionnaires" (discussed in the following paragraph) or as part of bona fide news reports. This includes candidates' statements to the media, to the general public, and to nonprofit organizations. The same applies to any statement volunteered by the candidate, even if a nonprofit has not solicited the statement. The candidate may distribute this statement at will, but the nonprofit may not.

### Questionnaires

Nonprofits with a broad range of concerns can safely disseminate responses from questionnaires. The questions must cover a broad range of subjects, be framed without bias, and be given to all candidates for office.

If a nonprofit has a very narrow focus, however, questionnaires may pose a problem. The Internal Revenue Service takes the position that a nonprofit's narrowness of focus implies endorsement of candidates whose replies are favorable to the questions posed. The same applies when candidates are asked to respond to a nonprofit's position paper. Unless you are certain that your organization clearly qualifies as covering a broad range of issues, your organization should avoid disseminating replies from questionnaires.

## Voting Records

Many nonprofits follow the useful practice of telling their members how each member of a legislature has voted on a key issue. This device shows who should be thanked and who needs to be persuaded and is a critically important tool in moving legislation forward. There is no legal problem with this practice, provided that if the information is presented and disseminated during the campaign it is done in the same manner as it is at other times. In presenting the results, it is important not to say "voted for us" or anything similar. Just say that the legislator voted for or against the measure. (The IRS has permitted the use of a plus (+) or a minus (-) to indicate whether a legislator has voted in accord with the organization's position.)

A problem arises if an organization waits to disseminate voting records until a campaign is under way. If your organization has followed the practice of disseminating voting records as votes occur throughout the year, then you are safe in publishing the record of a vote that occurs during a campaign. If, however, your organization has not published records regularly throughout the year, your group may not reach back during the campaign and publish a recap of the legislative votes throughout the legislative session. That is permissible, however, after the election.

## Public Forums

Nonprofits may invite candidates to meetings or to public forums sponsored by the organizations, in order to get the candidates' views on subjects of particular interest. The invitation must be extended to "all serious candidates." It is best to write to them all simultaneously and to use identical language in the invitations. It is not necessary that all candidates attend.

Even-handedness must be maintained in promoting and holding such a meeting or forum. The nonprofit should not state its views or comment on those of the candidates. If there is a question-and-answer period, each candidate must be given an equal opportunity to answer questions, and the moderator should strive to ensure balance.

Speeches or other remarks by candidates at the forum may be published as news items in the nonprofit's newsletter, if it is published regularly and if its circulation is limited to the organization's normal distribution patterns. All candidates must be given an equal opportunity to appear, and the news stories must be presented without editorial comment.

### Testimony On Party Platforms

As part of a lobbying effort, nonprofits may testify before party-platform committees at the national, state, or local levels of government. Responses to testimony may be reported in regularly published newsletters. Both parties' platform committees should receive copies of the testimony. Any account of the testimony and responses may be reported in a regularly scheduled publication.

### Issue Briefings and Candidates' Statements

Issue briefings for candidates must be extended to all the candidates running for a particular office. A candidate may publish a position paper or statement on the issue, but a nonprofit may not circulate the candidate's statement to the media, the general public, or the nonprofit's members.

### Membership Lists

The nonprofit may *sell, trade,* or *rent* its list to others, including candidates for office. If it does so, all candidates must be aware of the opportunity and be given the same access. An organization that *gives* or *lends* its membership list to a candidate is in effect making an illegal campaign contribution. To stay within the law, the nonprofit must be paid fair value in return.

### Indirect Lobbying Through a 501(c)(4) Organization

Some nonprofits have chosen to enlarge and strengthen their lobbying abilities by establishing 501(c)(4) organizations, thereby taking advantage of a 1983 U.S. Supreme Court decision. *Regan* v. *Taxation With Representation of Washington,* said that the First Amendment requires that nonprofits that are 501(c)(3) organizations be permitted to lobby indirectly through 501(c)(4) organizations.

Nonprofits—501(c)(3) organizations—are limited by law as to the amount they may spend on lobbying without penalty (see Chapter Nine). Organizations that are tax-exempt under Section 501(c)(4) do not have limitations on lobbying on behalf of their exempt purpose. Charitable contributions to 501(c)(4) organizations, however, are not tax-deductible.

Before the *Regan* v. *Taxation With Representation of Washington* decision, it had never been entirely clear to what extent a charity could control the actions of a lobbying affiliate. As a result of this uncertainty, very few nonprofits had set up 501(c)(4) organizations to indirectly broaden their lobbying outreach. The Supreme Court decision made clear that all the IRS can require by way of separation between a charity and its 501(c)(4) lobbying affiliate is "that the affiliate be separately incorporated" and that it "keep records adequate to show that tax-deductible contributions are not used to pay for lobbying" (*Regan* v. *Taxation With Representation of Washington,* 1983).

A charity can therefore control the activities of, and the legislative position taken by, its lobbying [501(c)(4)] affiliate. It is clear that a nonprofit and a 501(c)(4) affiliate may have identical priorities and boards of directors, and they may share personnel, office space, and facilities. In effect, a 501(c)(3) organization can set up and run a 501(c)(4) organization if the latter can raise its own hard money—that is, attract nondeductible contributions. The Supreme Court case should make the IRS very reluctant to push, on audit, the issue of a nonprofit's lobbying indirectly through a 501(c)(4) organization simply because the nonprofit controls it. But the 501(c)(4) organization must be run as a separate legal entity and must pay all its costs with nondeductible funds. The IRS can and does monitor that requirement closely. Therefore, it is important for the 501(c)(3) organization and the 501(c)(4) group to keep good records, showing that they properly divide costs for office space, staff time, equipment, and so on, so that the 501(c)(3) organization does not subsidize the 501(c)(4) organization.

For the vast majority of 501(c)(3) organizations, the 1976 lobby law provides all the lobbying latitude needed. Those groups that would like more lobbying conducted in their areas of interest should consider setting up a 501(c)(4) affiliate. Care will be needed, however, in keeping the two groups clearly separate, and contributors must be told that gifts to the affiliate are not deductible as charitable contributions.

### Individual and Political Action Committee (PAC) Contributions to Political Campaigns

A 501(c)(3) organization may not endorse, work for, pay the costs of, or otherwise support or oppose a candidate for public office. But, again, this in no way prohibits any of the nonprofit's officers, individual members, or employees from participating in elections, provided anything they say or do is done as private citizens and not as spokespersons for the nonprofit. If they choose to identify themselves with the organization, they must make it clear that they are speaking solely for themselves and not for the organization. If they do not identify themselves with the nonprofit but the media does, they have done nothing wrong.

Organizations that are tax-exempt under Section 501(c)(3) of the Internal Revenue Code are not permitted to establish political action committees (PACs). PACs are committees that raise or disburse money in federal election campaigns. They have become vehicles for the political involvement of supporters of unions, corporations, and other groups. PACs have been set up by a number of 501(c)(4) organizations. There is nothing to prohibit a 501(c)(3) from setting up a 501(c)(4), which in turn may set up a PAC, provided that the 501(c)(3) does not financially support either the 501(c)(4) or the PAC.

Under federal election law, 501(c)(4) groups cannot make contributions to federal candidates. Under recent Supreme Court rulings, however, (*Federal Election Commission* v. *Massachusetts Citizens for Life Inc., Dec. 15, 1986* and *Austin* v. *Michigan Chamber of Commerce, March 27, 1990*) a 501(c)(4) organization that gets no union or business money, operates entirely independently of any campaign, and meets other standards can make independent contributions for or against a candidate. Under those rulings, a 501(c)(4) organization is allowed to use dues and contributions for independent political spending without being obliged to establish a PAC and solicit funds for it separately. Direct contributions to federal candidates remain impermissible, as do coordinated efforts with a campaign. The independent expenditures must be reported to the Federal Election Commission. A 501(c)(4) organization that makes independent expenditures (or operates in a state that permits corporate contributions) is subject, under Internal Revenue Code Section 527, to taxation on its investment income, to the extent of its campaign expenditures and contributions.

### OMB Circular A-122—Restrictions on Nonprofits That Lobby and Receive Federal Funds

Federal restrictions prohibiting some nonprofits from using any federal funds for lobbying were issued by the Office of Management and Budget (OMB) on April 25, 1984. The rules permit nonprofits to use federal dollars to carry out some legislation-related activities that are not defined as lobbying under OMB Circular A-122.

*General Provisions*

As a condition of obtaining federal funds, nonprofits are required by OMB to make certain that none of those funds are used for lobbying, as defined by OMB. It is the responsibility of the federal agency making the award to ensure that the nonprofit complies with the federal rules. Before receiving the funds, the nonprofit has the right to meet with the awarding federal agency and to be told what costs will be allowable. That should help a nonprofit clarify, from the outset, any ambiguity about expenditures of federal funds for legislative activity.

*Who Is Covered?*

OMB Circular A-122, "Cost Principles for Nonprofit Organizations," to which lobbying regulations have been added as a new
paragraph—B-21 of Attachment B—applies to some nonprofits, including those that receive subgrants and subcontracts. Included (in
part) are nonprofits that operate primarily for scientific, educational, service, charitable, or similar purposes in the public interest;
are not organized primarily for profit; and use their net proceeds to
maintain and provide or expand their operations. Those not covered include colleges and universities. They are covered by OMB
Circular A-21, which does not mention lobbying. Hospitals are covered under U.S. Department of Health and Human Services publication *A Guide for Hospitals: Cost Principles and Procedures for
Establishing Indirect Costs and Patient Care Rates for Grants and
Contracts with HEW*. Lobbying is not mentioned in that document.

*What Is Lobbying?*

The OMB limitation on lobbying applies only to lobbying at the
federal and state levels, not at the local level. OMB defines direct and
grass-roots lobbying separately but makes no distinction between
them in applying sanctions. Direct lobbying is "any attempt to
influence (i) the introduction of federal or state legislation; or (ii)
the enactment or modification of any pending federal or state legislation through communication with any member or employee of
the Congress or state legislature (including efforts to influence state
or local officials to engage in similar lobbying activity), or with any
government official in connection with a decision to sign or veto
enrolled legislation." Grass-roots lobbying is "any attempt to influence (i) the introduction of federal or state legislation; or (ii) the
enactment or modification of any pending federal or state legislation by preparing, distributing, or using publicity or propaganda
or by urging members of the general public or any segment thereof
to contribute or participate in any mass demonstration, march,
rally, fund-raising, lobbying campaign, or letter or telephone campaign." The OMB's definition of lobbying also includes "legisla-

tive liaison activities, including attendance at legislative sessions or committee hearings, gathering information regarding legislation, and analyzing the affected legislation, when such activities are in support of or in knowing preparation for an effort to engage in unallowable lobbying." "Knowing preparation" is not defined, but OMB explains that its inclusion should "avoid unintended retroactivity problems by not permitting auditors to automatically disallow legislative costs in every instance where they are associated with later efforts at lobbying." Apparently, nonprofits will not be held accountable by OMB if they participate in legislative liaison activities without the knowledge that, later on, they will use the information gained from those activities in lobbying.

### Political Activity

Among its unallowable lobbying activities, OMB includes "attempts to influence the outcome of any federal, state, local election, referendum, initiative, or similar procedure" and "supporting any political party or any other organization established for the purpose of influencing the outcomes of elections."

### What Is Not Lobbying?

OMB exempts

> providing a technical and factual presentation on a topic directly related to the performance of a grant, contract, or other agreement through hearing testimony, statements or letters to Congress, or a state legislature, or subdivision, member, or cognizant staff member, in response to a documented request (including a *Congressional Record* notice requesting testimony or statements for the record at a regularly scheduled hearing) made by the recipient member, legislative body or subdivision, or a cognizant staff member thereof; provided such information is readily

obtainable and can be readily put into deliverable
form; and further provided that costs under the section
for travel, lodging, or meals are unallowable unless
incurred to offer testimony at a regularly scheduled
Congressional hearing, pursuant to written request
for such presentation made by the Chairman Ranking
Minority member of the Committee or Subcommittee
conducting such hearing.

Also excluded from lobbying are efforts to influence state
legislation in order to directly reduce the costs or avoid material
impairment of the organization's authority to perform the grant,
contract, or agreement. In explanation of this provision, OMB em-
phasizes that the exception relates to an organization's authority
and not to its ability to perform. Lobbying for the purpose of im-
proving performance is not exempt.

The regulations seem to say, for example, that a sharp de-
crease in a state appropriation for a program provided by a particular nonprofit could affect the nonprofit's ability to perform, but
the nonprofit could not use federal funds to lobby for the appropriation. Nevertheless, it apparently could use federal funds to lobby
the state legislature to protect its authority to perform the grant,
contract, or agreement.

OMB also excludes from its definition of lobbying "any activity specifically authorized by statute to be undertaken with funds
from the grant, contract, or other agreement." Some nonprofits are
currently authorized to lobby for particular programs, and this provision is clearly intended to avoid changing that authority.

### Amount of Lobbying Permitted

OMB places no restrictions on the amount of lobbying that may be
undertaken, as long as none of the lobbying costs, either direct or
indirect, are met with funds obtained through a federal grant or
contract, subgrant, or subcontract.

*Record Keeping and Reporting*

OMB requires charities to maintain adequate records and refers them to its Circular A-110 as a source of further information.

To ensure that activities funded by federal awards do not bear more than their fair share of *indirect costs* (managers' salaries, support services, utilities, and so on), the nonprofit organization annually negotiates with the awarding federal agency the manner in which indirect costs are to be determined and allocated. An organization receiving grants, contracts, or subawards from more than one agency negotiates with the agency that is making the largest dollar volume of awards and then applies the results to the awards from other agencies.

In advance of other negotiation, the organization submits a formal proposal, which forms the basis for negotiation. Any gray areas between organization and agency are resolved during negotiation and may not be reopened during audit.

A nonprofit's indirect-cost proposal must identify total lobbying costs to be included during the award. Thus lobbying conducted by a nonprofit with its private funds must be identified.

Each direct-cost employee who expects to allocate more than 25 percent of his or her time to lobbying or lobbying support during any month is required to keep a time log for that month.

*Penalties for Violation*

The OMB explanation that accompanies Circular A-122 states that penalties for violating lobbying restrictions are the same as those for violating other restrictions in Circular A-122. The major sanction for minor or unintentional violations is cost recovery. In more serious cases, contracts or grants may be suspended or terminated, or contractors and grantees may be barred from further awards.

## Lobbying with Private Foundation Grants and Corporate Contributions

Nonprofits are not disqualified from lobbying because they receive foundation funds, but nonprofits and, even more, foundations have been slow to recognize and act on this fact. While grant funds from a private foundation to a nonprofit must not be earmarked for lobbying, it is perfectly legal for the nonprofit to use unearmarked foundation funds to lobby. Foundation funds are considered to be earmarked only if there has been an oral or written agreement that the grant will be used for specific purposes. If there is no oral or written agreement and the nonprofit controls how the grant funds are used, then it may lobby with those general-purpose grant dollars.

The IRS regulations have set up a highly protective system for grants by private foundations to charities that lobby. The regulations apply to all grants for public charities, and they should remove any remaining uncertainty among foundations about granting funds to nonprofits that elect to come under the 1976 lobby law. Under these rules, a foundation may, without incurring a penalty tax, make a general-purpose grant to a public charity that lobbies and may make a grant to support a specific project that includes lobbying, as long as its own grant is less than the amount budgeted for the nonlobbying parts of the project. For example (to repeat a scenario described in Chapter Nine), if a specific project has a $200,000 budget, of which $20,000 is to be spent for lobbying, then a private foundation may give the project up to $180,000 (the part of the project budget allocated to nonlobbying uses). The fact that other private foundations have already made grants for the project need not be taken into account in considering how much a private foundation can give. See Chapter Nine for a more detailed discussion.

The regulations make clear that the foundation can rely on statements by the prospective grantee as to the lobbying budget for a project, unless it knows or has reason to know that the statements are false. The regulations also make clear that, so long as the grantor foundation complies with these standards when it makes the grant, it will not be held to have made a taxable lobbying expenditure because the public charity violates the assurances it gave when seeking the grant.

There are other important areas associated with legislation that are not considered lobbying, where it is permissible for nonprofits to use earmarked foundation funds. They include nonpartisan analysis or research and provision of technical advice or assistance to a governmental or legislative body in response to a written request from that body. Nonprofits may devote an unlimited amount of their activity to providing such technical advice or assistance to a governmental or legislative body in response to a written request from that body, and they can provide nonpartisan analysis or research even though such matters relate to pending legislation. All of that activity may be fully funded by foundations.

The IRS regulations are also clear that a nonprofit may use foundation funds to furnish results of analysis or research on legislative issues, if it presents the facts fully and fairly enough so that the audience can form independent opinions. The regulations make clear that research and analysis need not be neutral or objective to fall within this nonpartisan exclusion. The exclusion also covers research or analysis that takes a direct position on the merits of legislation, as long as the organization presents facts fully and fairly, makes the material generally available, and does not include a direct call to the reader to contact legislators.

Nonprofits that have elected to come under the 1976 lobby law have occasionally found that foundations have been "scared off" by the fact that the nonprofit has elected to come under the provisions of that legislation. Some foundations fear that a general purpose grant to a nonprofit that has elected might make them subject to a tax penalty. The IRS regulations, which codified a 1977 letter ruling to the McIntosh Foundation, make clear that such fears are unfounded. The regulations hold that general-support grants to nonprofits that have elected to come under the 1976 lobby law (like those nonprofits that have not elected) do not constitute taxable expenditures if the grants are not earmarked, and if there is no written or oral agreement that the nonprofit will use the grants for specific lobbying purposes. Regulations based on the McIntosh Ruling should allay any remaining fears of foundations regarding general purpose grants to nonprofits that elect.

Nonprofits may receive grants earmarked for lobbying from community foundations. Community foundations are tax-exempt under Section 501(c)(3) of the Internal Revenue Code and are not treated as private foundations so they are permitted the same lobbying latitude as other nonprofits. For example, a community foundation that has elected to come under the 1976 lobby law may spend funds to lobby. It may also grant earmarked funds to a nonprofit group for lobbying, up to the limits permitted by law. A community foundation's grant, earmarked for lobbying, would count against the community foundation's own lobbying ceiling. A community foundation may receive earmarked personal funds for lobbying only if the funds are not deducted by the donor from his or her taxes.

There are other important ways in which private foundation funds can be used to lobby. Foundations may fund self-defense direct lobbying by a nonprofit. Such lobbying includes lobbying on legislation that may affect the existence of the nonprofit, its powers and duties, its tax-exempt status, and the tax-deductibility of the contributions it receives. For example, the lobbying that has been conducted by nonprofits in support of charitable-contribution tax deductions is self-defense lobbying, and so foundations may fund that activity. Lobbying for government appropriations that would be received by the nonprofit is not self-defense lobbying.

There is much more latitude for making grants to nonprofits that lobby than many believe. A number of foundations have liberalized their policies for granting funds to nonprofits that lobby, and nonprofits are well served by this enlightened view.

Nonprofits have never actively pursued corporations to fund lobbying activities, although a growing number of corporations are supporting nonprofits that lobby aggressively for their causes and clients. A nonprofit may use corporate or personal contributions to lobby if the contributions are *not* earmarked for lobbying. It appears that corporations, like foundations, may also provide earmarked funds for self-defense lobbying by nonprofits, although the law is not entirely clear on this matter.

## Reporting Lobbying Expenditures to the IRS

Organizations that lobby (except churches, associations of churches, and integrated auxiliaries) are required to report their lobbying expenditures to the IRS on Form 990. Record keeping and reporting requirements for organizations that elect to come under the 1976 lobby law are somewhat different from requirements for those that fall under the substantiality test. For electing organizations they are, if anything, simpler.

All nonprofits, whether they elect or not, have to report annually to the IRS how much they spend on lobbying. The only additional information required of electing organizations is to calculate their ceilings and state how much of their lobbying is grassroots; for example, aimed at getting the general public to lobby legislators. Electing organizations, unlike those subject to the substantiality test, are not required to include detailed descriptions of their lobbying activities.

Both types of organizations do have to maintain records. If they are audited, they will be required to substantiate what they have reported on Form 990. Electing and nonelecting organizations need systems for recording how much they spend on lobbying.

The IRS will accept any reasonable method of doing this. For example, you may use a sampling, instead of complete time records, to estimate how much time your staff spends on lobbying activity. If the sample periods are generally representative of how you use most of your time, you might want to pick out a two-week period each quarter and keep track of your activities, in thirty-minute segments, to determine how much of your activities constitutes lobbying. In estimating your lobbying expenditures each quarter, you would simply make adjustments on the basis of your in-depth two-week assessments. Overhead costs related to your lobbying expenditures must also be reported.

The main point is that you should make a good-faith effort to keep track of your lobbying expenditures. You may want to develop a form, which would include such information as the date, the nature of the activity (visit with a legislator, development of an action alert, telephone calls to your members urging action), and whether it represented direct or grass-roots lobbying. The extent to which you want to keep a regular record of your lobbying activities will depend on how representative your sample assessment is and on whether you can make reasonably close general estimates from that assessment without keeping more detailed records.

## Registering as a Lobbyist for a Nonprofit

It is questionable whether staff members who lobby at the federal level for nonprofits are required to register under the 1946 Federal Regulation of Lobbying Act, as modified in 1954. The 1946 law requires any individual who receives monetary compensation from any person or group for the purpose of lobbying Congress to register with the clerk of the House of Representatives and the secretary of the Senate. Other requirements include filing quarterly reports with the House and Senate, disclosing lobbying expenses, identifying the lobbyist's employer, and giving the general legislative objectives of the organization. The law includes misdemeanor penalties for violation of the disclosure provisions.

A 1954 Supreme Court decision sharply narrowed the focus and applicability of the 1946 Federal Regulation of Lobbying Act in a way that seems to remove the obligation of nonprofits to register. The court's decision makes the 1946 registration law applicable only to groups or individuals whose principal activities are "directed in substantial part" to influencing legislation through direct contacts with members of Congress but not members' staffs. Several other findings in the 1954 decision also seem to rule out the need for at least some nonprofits to register. For example, the decision also held that an individual or group is not subject to the law if the only lobbying conducted is grass-roots lobbying or contacting staffs of members. An individual working for nonprofits does have to register if all the following conditions exist:

1. The person must have solicited, collected, or received contributions.
2. One of the person's main purposes, or one of the main purposes of the contributions, must have been to influence the passage or defeat of legislation by Congress.
3. The intended method of accomplishing this purpose must have been through direct communication with members of Congress.

Information for nonprofits that do want to register can be found in Resource F.

All states and many local governments, like the federal government, also have laws regulating lobbying. These laws vary widely in their requirements for registration, reporting, and record keeping. State lobby laws may be administered and enforced by special commissions, a state attorney general's office, or other agencies. Most also levy fines and enforce sanctions for violations.

# Resource A

# Lobbying by Nonprofits: A Checklist

Lobbying isn't a very complicated process. If you can pick up a pen or a phone, you can lobby. This checklist will help you skim quickly through the main subjects covered by this book and know what will be most helpful to you. While you are skimming, keep in mind that most how-to books, including this one, tell you much more than you'll ever need to know about how to get the job done.

### You Need to Know Only a *Little* About the Following to Get Started Lobbying (Chapter 1)

1. The legislative process
2. Organizing your group's government relations committee
3. Setting up a legislative network
4. The law governing lobbying by nonprofits

### The Nonprofit Lobbyist's Skills and the Legislative Process (Chapter Two)

1. You don't need a paid lobbyist—a volunteer lobbyist can do the job.
2. What your lobbyist needs and needs to know
   - A few basics about the legislative process
   - Several main arguments for the bill you are supporting

- Your group's organizational structure and how it communicates with its grass roots
3. Strong interpersonal skills

### Selecting Your Leader in the Legislature (Chapter Two)

1. You'll need a strong advocate for your bill in the legislative
   committee that has jurisdiction over your legislation
2. Skills and commitment of the legislative staff person assigned
   to your measure

### The Legislative Process (Chapter Two)

1. The legislative process is controlled by people, not by
   institutions.
2. In both chambers of a legislature, legislation usually moves
   from subcommittee to full committee to a floor vote, and then
   to conference between the two chambers. At each step of the
   process, it is possible to influence the outcome of the legislation, but the best chance is at the subcommittee level.
3. All members of a legislature are not equal. Majority party
   members have more power than minority members. Senior
   members are usually more influential than newer members.
4. The legislative process is run by people. Put yourself in your
   legislator's shoes.
5. Don't take a legislator's vote against your proposal personally.
   Maybe the legislator will be with you next time.
6. Staff people are important. Senior staff people may wield enormous power. They can assist you greatly in guiding your legislation to enactment.

### Lobbying the Administration (Chapter Two)

1. Your group's success in enacting legislation can be lost
   through restrictive regulations.
2. Nonprofits often have modest influence on the executive
   branch when lobbying them directly, but the executive branch
   can be moved with the aid of legislators.

3. Media support for your position, and criticism in the media of the government's position, can have an enormous impact.

### Effective Written Communications (Chapter Three)

1. Be *accurate*. You, your legislator, and your cause all lose from the fallout of inaccurate information.
2. Be *brief*. Almost no one wants to read more than one page.
3. Be *clear*. Even those who are new to your subject shouldn't have to struggle to understand your communication.
4. Be *timely*. Your communication must arrive with sufficient lead time for grass-roots recipients to contact legislators before a vote.
5. Follow up with a telephone call. Most people don't respond to written communications without a follow-up call.

### Grass-Roots Action Through a Legislative Network (Chapter Four)

1. A grass-roots network is an organized, systematic means of communicating on short notice with volunteers at the local level who have agreed to contact their legislators on behalf of your issue.
2. Grass-roots networks don't have to be elaborate.
3. Volunteers are more influential with legislators than nonprofit staff are.
4. Setting up a network
   - Get a list of legislators you want to contact.
   - Recruit volunteers who can establish contact with those legislators.
   - Develop a means of communicating very quickly with members of your network, including telephone calls.
   - Work at it. Networks are absolutely essential, but they atrophy quickly if you do not give them top priority.

### Highly Effective Lobbying Techniques and Communications (Chapter Five)

1. Site visits by legislators
2. Personal visits by constituents

3. Spontaneous, individually composed letters from constituents
4. Telephone calls from constituents
5. Articles in major daily newspapers
6. Editorials in major daily newspapers

### Letters to Legislators (Chapter Five)

1. Write on your personal or business letterhead.
2. Keep your letter to one page, and put your message in your own words.
3. Ask the legislator to reply, and ask very directly whether he or she will support your position.
4. Like everyone else, legislators don't like a threatening tone.
5. Don't overstate your organization's influence.
6. Be certain that your legislator receives your letter before the vote.
7. Thank the legislator.

### Meeting with Your Legislator (Chapter Five)

1. You may be nervous, but remember that you probably know more about the subject than the legislator does.
2. Make an appointment.
3. It's acceptable to bring a delegation.
4. Discuss your issue from the legislator's perspective.
5. If you can't answer a question, don't bluff.
6. Leave a fact sheet.
7. Write to say thanks and to remind the legislator of agreements reached.

### Presenting Testimony (Chapter Five)

1. Keep your statement brief, and provide a one-page summary.
2. A high-ranking, well-informed volunteer should be the presenter. A senior staff member is a second choice.
3. Get other groups to sign your testimony.
4. Plant questions with friendly legislators.
5. Oral statements should not be read.

6. It's perfectly acceptable to be direct in your response to a hostile question, but be courteous.
7. If you can't answer a question, say so, and offer to get the information.

### Telephoning Your Legislator Regarding
### a Vote (Chapter Five)

1. If you can get through, a telephone call can be very persuasive.
2. Keep your call brief.
3. If you can't get through to the legislator, ask for the aide assigned to the issue.
4. If you can't reach the aide, leave your message with the person who answered the phone.
5. Calls to the district office of a legislator are second best but much better than nothing.

### Other Ways to Communicate with Legislators (Chapter Five)

1. Invite them to visit your facility
2. Have legislators speak at a public meeting sponsored by your organization
3. Invite legislators to meet with your board of directors
4. Sponsor a breakfast meeting at the Capitol

### Lobbying in Coalition (Chapter Six)

1. Almost all major legislation is enacted as a result of coalitions' efforts.
2. Coalitions are always fragile but have a potentially enormous influence over legislation.
3. A main function of coalition leaders is to build a sense of trust and openness, with honesty and "no surprises" paramount.
4. Every coalition must have an organization that serves as a clearinghouse.
5. The clearinghouse function—getting information to coalition members quickly—is critically important.
6. Coalition membership may change markedly over time, de-

pending on other issues important to some of your coalition's members.

7.  In coalition action, it can take as many as four steps in the process to get information from the coalition to the person being asked to take action at the grassroots, so plan carefully.

8.  When a coalition effort is successful, make certain that all members are aware of the important role they played in the success.

### Key Points About a Government Relations Committee (Chapter Seven)

1.  The biggest mistake made by government relations committees of nonprofits is to take on more than one top priority.

2.  The committee can have twenty issues on its priority list, but all must be ranked.

3.  A committee member may push the staff hard to emphasize his or her pet priority, even though the committee has decided otherwise. Don't give in.

4.  The committee should delegate authority to a small group for decisions on legislation when time doesn't permit consultation with the parent group.

5.  The committee should broadly represent the organization's constituency.

6.  According to the size of the organization, much of the government relations committee's work should be delegated to task forces or other subgroups.

7.  At meetings, pay attention to process:
    *   Agendas are important.
    *   Set a cordial tone.
    *   Pay attention to the physical arrangements of the table and the meeting room.
    *   Don't let the chair, the staff, or anyone else dominate.
    *   Save everyone embarrassment by using name tent cards at each place.

### Lobbying Through the Media (Chapter Eight)

1.  Legislators take note of organizations that the media quote in news stories on key legislative issues.

2.  Congressional staff rank news articles and editorials in daily newspapers very high as forces that influence members of Congress.
3.  A person with experience in media relations (he or she may be a volunteer) can save your group much time by helping you target your media efforts.
4.  Points to keep in mind
    *   Send only newsworthy information to the media.
    *   There is a herd instinct in the media, which can help your media campaign snowball if you get one story in the influential media.
    *   Reporters look for quotable sources. Have your off-the-cuff remarks well rehearsed.
    *   Keep a list of media people who have contacted you or written or spoken on your issue—they represent a future resource gold mine!
    *   A press release should give the most important information in the first paragraph, and the rest in descending order of importance. The first page of the release should answer *who, what, when, where,* and *why.*
5.  Press conferences
    *   In most major metropolitan areas, it is difficult to get good press conference attendance because there are always so many competing issues.
    *   Know the hour and day that the press are most likely to attend.
    *   Know the location that will attract reporters.
    *   Know how far in advance the press must be notified and how best to do so.
    *   Give a reminder call on the day of the press conference.
    *   Have a well-written press statement and background.
    *   Be certain that your audio system is flawless.
    *   Keep it short, and leave time for questions.
    *   Keep a list of attendees for follow-up.
6.  Letters to the editor
    *   Keep the letter tightly composed.
    *   Use specific examples.
    *   Address one point per letter.

- Use accurate, up-to-date information.
- Don't attack the opposition.
- Always sign your name, and include your address and telephone number.

7. Radio and television
    - Radio and television still offer public service time.
    - Don't forget news directors of radio and television stations when circulating your press release.
    - It helps greatly to have a visual angle for your television news story.
    - Keep your public service spots short: for TV, nine to ten seconds; for radio, twenty to thirty seconds.
    - Get a well-briefed spokesperson for your group on a radio or television talk show.
    - Give local radio or television your ideas for editorials.

# Resource B

## Questions and Answers Regarding the Law and Lobbying by Nonprofits

1. *Q:* Is lobbying legal? (Chapter Nine)

   *A:* It's not only legal but also encouraged by Congress and the IRS.

2. *Q:* How much can I spend on lobbying? (Chapter Nine)

   *A:* A generous amount: 20 percent of your organization's first $500,000 of annual expenditures, 15 percent of next $500,000, 10 percent of the next $500,000, and so on, up to $1 million.

3. *Q:* Can all nonprofits spend that much? (Chapter Nine)

   *A:* No, only those that elect.

4. *Q:* Elect what? (Chapter Nine)

   *A:* Elect to come under the generous provisions of the 1976 lobby law.

5. *Q:* How do I elect? (Chapter Nine)

   *A:* It's simple. Have your organization's governing body vote to come under the 1976 law and file IRS form 5768.

6. *Q:* Will the IRS "red flag" us for audit if we elect the lobby law? (Chapter Nine)

   *A:* Absolutely not. The IRS has made that clear.

7. *Q:* That's all there is to it? (Chapter Nine)

   *A:* Yes. Sign IRS Form 5768, and send it to the IRS.

### The "Insubstantial" Rule (Chapter Nine)

1.  *Q:* What if we don't elect?
    *A:* You are subject to the vague "insubstantial" rule.
2.  *Q:* What does the "insubstantial rule" mean?
    *A:* If you engage in "more than insubstantial" lobbying, you lose the right to receive tax-deductible contributions and lose your exemption.
3.  *Q:* What is "more than insubstantial"?
    *A:* That's not clear. Several court decisions have addressed the definitions.
4.  *Q:* What did the courts find?
    *A:* In 1955, that 5 percent of total activities is not substantial; in 1974, that each case must be evaluated according to "facts and circumstances"; and in 1972, that a percentage test is inappropriate, since a single official position statement could be considered substantial.
5.  *Q:* How can I avoid this confusion?
    *A:* Elect to come under the 1976 lobby law.

### What Is Lobbying Under the 1976 Lobby Law?
### (Chapter Nine)

1.  *Q:* If I elect to come under the 1976 lobby law, which of my activities will be lobbying?
    *A:* Any attempt to influence any legislation through communication with any member or employee of a legislative body or with any government official or employee who may participate in the formulation of the legislation (called *direct lobbying*), and any attempt to influence any legislation through an attempt to affect the opinions of the general public or any segment thereof (called *grass-roots lobbying*).
2.  *Q:* Can you make that less confusing?
    *A:* Maybe. Direct lobbying occurs when a nonprofit organization (including its members who reside at the grass roots) contacts a policymaker on behalf of legislation. You are

doing direct lobbying in your communications only if you refer to specific legislation and reflect a view of its merits. Grass-roots lobbying occurs when a nonprofit organization contacts the general public and urges people to contact policymakers in support of legislation. You are doing grass-roots *lobbying* if, in communicating with the general public, you refer to specific legislation, reflect a view of its merits, and encourage the general public to contact legislators.

3.  *Q:* May I spend all of my total allowable lobbying expenditures on grass-roots lobbying?

    *A:* No. Only 25 percent may be spent on grass-roots lobbying.

4.  *Q:* Is there a similar limitation on direct lobbying?

    *A:* No. You may spend 100 percent of allowable expenditures on direct lobbying.

5.  *Q:* How do the new IRS regulations affect lobbying?

    *A:* They provide helpful details regarding what is and is not treated as direct and grass-roots lobbying.

6.  *Q:* What are some other key issues covered by the lobbying regulations?

    *A:* For grass-roots lobbying, there is a special rule for paid mass-media messages. The regulations also define when materials developed in the previous six months and used in lobbying are a lobbying expenditure. They also explain how to allocate the costs of a communication that includes both a lobbying and a nonlobbying expenditure. They make clear when nonpartisan analysis study or research is not a lobbying expenditure.

7.  *Q:* Is that all I need to know about the regulations?

    *A:* It depends. If you plan to do what you consider extensive lobbying, you should read Chapter Nine. If your lobbying is limited, simply keep in mind that the lobbying latitude under the law is generous.

## Other Lobbying Limits (Chapter Ten)

1.  *Q:* What is self-defense lobbying?

    *A:* Lobbying on legislation affecting the existence of the organization itself, its powers and duties, its tax-exempt status, or the deductibility of contributions to it.

2.  *Q:* What are the limits on self-defense lobbying?

    *A:* There are no limits on self-defense direct lobbying. Grassroots lobbying isn't protected by the self-defense provision.

3.  *Q:* What are examples of self-defense lobbying?

    *A:* Lobbying in support of charitable-contribution tax deductions or to change the law regarding lobbying rights of nonprofits.

### Voter Education by Nonprofits
### (Chapter Ten)

1.  *Q:* May nonprofits carry out voter education during a political campaign?

    *A:* Yes, if it is strictly nonpartisan.

2.  *Q:* What kind of voter education is legal?

    *A:* It's legal to inform candidates of your position. If the candidate goes on record on your issue, the candidate may distribute the statement, but you may not. You may distribute the answers to a nonpartisan questionnaire and hold nonpartisan forums.

3.  *Q:* What about questionnaires to candidates?

    *A:* A nonprofit can disseminate responses from questionnaires, but the questions must cover a broad range of concerns, be framed without bias, and be given to all the candidates for an office.

4.  *Q:* What about distributing voting records of candidates?

    *A:* You may, if you distribute voting records throughout the year and not just during the campaign.

5.  *Q:* May I invite candidates to a public forum to get their views?

    *A:* Yes, if you invite all candidates, are evenhanded, don't state your views or comment on candidates' views; and give all candidates the opportunity to answer questions.

6.  *Q:* May I publish information from the forum?

    *A:* Yes, in your newsletter, if it is published regularly, and if its circulation is limited to your organization's members. Candidates should also be given equal opportunity to reply.

## Foundations and Nonprofits' Lobbying
### (Chapter Ten)

1. *Q:* May nonprofits use private foundation grants to lobby?
   *A:* Private foundation grants that are awarded for general purposes may be used by nonprofits to lobby, but earmarked funds may not be used.
2. *Q:* May nonprofits use community foundation grants to lobby?
   *A:* Nonprofits may receive grants from community foundations that *are* earmarked for lobbying.

## Other Issues
### (Chapter Ten)

1. *Q:* Is urging voters to put a proposal (an initiative) on a ballot lobbying?
   *A:* Yes, it's direct lobbying.
2. *Q:* Is urging members of a legislature to put a law passed by the legislature (referendum) on the ballot lobbying?
   *A:* Yes, it's direct lobbying.
3. *Q:* Can a Section 501(c)(3) organization lobby indirectly through a 501(c)(4) organization?
   *A:* Yes.
4. *Q:* Why consider such an arrangement?
   *A:* A 501(c)(4) organization may spend all of its funds on lobbying—but contributions to it aren't tax-deductible.
5. *Q:* Are there any cautions regarding such an arrangement?
   *A:* Keep good records that show clearly how staff time, equipment, office space, costs, and so on, are divided between the groups, and be sure the (c)(3) doesn't provide financial support to the (c)(4).
6. *Q:* May a 501(c)(3) organization set up a political action committee (PAC)?
   *A:* No.

7.  *Q:* May a 501(c)(4) set up a PAC?
    *A:* Yes.
8.  *Q:* May nonprofits use federal funds to lobby?
    *A:* No, with the exception of lobbying specifically authorized by federal law.
9.  *Q:* May nonprofits use federal funds to provide technical assistance?
    *A:* Yes, if requested to do so by legislators.
10. *Q:* May they use federal funds for self-defense lobbying?
    *A:* Yes—for example, to avoid material impairment of the organization's authority to perform with respect to a grant, a contract, or an agreement.
11. *Q:* How are lobbying expenditures reported to the IRS?
    *A:* On IRS Form 990A Schedule.
12. *Q:* Must nonprofits that don't elect to come under the 1976 law report lobbying expenditures to the IRS?
    *A:* Yes.
13. *Q:* Must nonprofits' lobbyists register?
    *A:* Yes, under some rather narrow conditions.
14. *Q:* How does one register as a lobbyist?
    *A:* By contacting the secretary of the United States Senate or the clerk of the U.S. House of Representatives.

# Resource C

## "How to Win
## the Advocacy Game:
## Rarified Air," by Doug Siglin

*"You can lead these horses to water, but it's a lot harder to make 'em pass legislation."*
*Doug's favorite hill staffer*

I've been thinking a lot about trying to explain this business of successful issue advocacy with Congress.

Last night, as I watched my college alma mater play basketball on TV, a simple idea came to me. Although sports analogies are usually too facile to be of much real use, I'm going to put this one out for your consideration.

Here it is: successful basketball teams have to be able to play both a good *inside* and a good *outside* game. So do groups that are consistently successful at working with Congress.

In basketball, the inside game is generally the purview of the centers and forwards. They block off the middle of the court, reject opposing shots, get rebounds, and make the high percentage of field goals from under the basket. The outside game generally belongs to the guards. They pressure the other team, direct the offense, and make those 15–20 foot jumpers look easy. A team which doesn't have both good inside and good outside games may win, but it won't be consistently good.

Originally published by InterAction as part of their Monday Developments Series: 1989, 7 (3). Reprinted with permission.

In the congressional case, there is also an inside game and an outside game. The inside game is building trusting relationships, learning how the situation looks from those most intimate with it, and getting voluntary help. The outside game is "pressuring" members of Congress. The two must go together in order to win consistently.

## The Inside Game

Despite the general impression to the contrary, being a member of Congress is an outrageously tough job. Most members are on the go six or seven days a week from sunrise to long past sunset. They are continually being asked to do things for people they barely know or don't know at all. They have groups of constituents to meet in their offices or take to the Capitol steps for pictures. They have dozens of joint committees, standing committees, select committees, subcommittees, state delegation, special caucus, and task force meetings to attend, usually simultaneously. They have to stay awake and look interested through boring technical hearings on arcane matters.

Moreover, they have to be continually dealing with the press and prepared to dispense witty new pearls of wisdom to groups during breakfasts, lunches, and dinners. They have to answer letters, make military academy nominations, write dozens of recommendation letters, battle with federal agencies, and fly back to their districts as often as they can hack it. They have to manage dual, triple, or quadruple offices and staffs, two residences, and their own families. They have to mind their political P's and Q's or they will find themselves jobless. And perhaps most annoying, they have to withstand constant abuse and have to be perpetually vigilant about what they say, even at their tiredest, crankiest moments. Just in terms of the energy it takes to be a member of Congress, these people are heroes.

When asked to take a position or some action on any given issue, a member of Congress will probably base a decision on a mix of at least six factors: (1) who is asking; (2) what they personally want to do; (3) what is good for the people they represent; (4) what is good national policy; (5) what is politically realistic; and (6) what won't get them rudely unelected. Staff have to make similar sorts of judgments, taking all these things into consideration on behalf of their bosses, plus some other factors of their own, like their positions in the office and how much the boss delegates.

Being human, members of Congress and staff are far more inclined to try to work with people over time who are more than just a letter or a phone call—particularly people who understand the other five parts of the mix and tailor their requests accordingly. They are likely to give such people the straightforward information that is such a valuable commodity. And if the member of Congress one has built a trusting relationship with is a committee chair or has some other high-ranking position, important doors can be opened with a very few words.

The bottom line on the inside game is this: if you establish honest relationships with members of Congress and their staffs and respect the limitations they face, they'll be far more inclined to *voluntarily* give you a hand.

### The Outside Game

The outside game is the pressure individuals and groups can put on members of Congress to somewhat less voluntarily do what is wanted.

The pressure game comes in many forms, but in the end it comes down to this: making members of Congress fear that they won't get reelected. Members of Congress almost always want to get re-elected (and more than 95 percent of them do). They often begin thinking about the next election well before the current one is wrapped up.

There is a lot of attention today about the role of money in politics, but the question of money is almost always ultimately a question of votes. Campaigns have become fantastically expensive—it's said that the average senator has to raise $10,000 dollars every working day to get reelected. Money equals TV time and billboards and yard signs and rallies and photo opportunities, and those equal votes. Groups that have lots of cash can play a great outside game.

But even those who don't have money can play a pressure game. The hunger lobbying groups RESULTS has figured out a

wonderful way to do this. It gets its supporters to convince local
newspaper editorial boards to write editorials about hunger, and
then it sends reams of them to members of Congress. It's a wonderful and original pressure technique, and it has been quite effective. Other pressure techniques are letters . . . postcards, citizen
press events and rallies, newspaper advertisements, and the like.

These outside game techniques get the attention of members
of Congress, and if large or impressive enough can make them fear
for their careers—and subsequently pay far more attention to the
issues driving the pressure.

Last week's pay raise fiasco was a unique but interesting
example of pressure. I don't think many lessons can be drawn from
the case because of the intense public outrage at a 51 percent pay
increase in a time of budget cuts, but do you know what eventually
made the House change its collective mind? Tens of thousands of
*tea bags!*

Here's what I think the point of all this is: both the inside
game and the outside game are critical. Members will often respond
to pressure techniques—particularly members who are less "safe" in
their seats—but they do so unwillingly. Moreover, the "movers and
shakers" have safe seats or they wouldn't be where they are. There
are practical limitations to what pressure can do.

On the other hand, the *inside game* depends on an ability to
establish a trusting relationship with members or their staffs: something which is often critical in the case of key individuals but isn't
practical for all 538 members of Congress. This is also a limitation.

Just like basketball teams, nongovernmental organizations
[NGOs] need to play both games to win consistently. RESULTS
has invented a good outside technique and uses it effectively but
doesn't have much inside game and therefore loses critical support
of important players and makes unneeded mistakes. Other NGOs
have a pretty good inside game but need to develop ways to work
up a little pressure—or at least the threat of it. Letters, postcards,
and the like would help a lot to achieve the ultimate end.

Last night, my team lost by one point in double overtime
because the other team got a combinaton of (outside) three-point
baskets and a game winning (inside) lay-up. I think there really is
a lesson here.

Do NGOs have both the inside and the outside skills it takes to consistently win in this congressional advocacy game?

*Doug Siglin is public policy director for InterAction.*

# Resource D

## Examples of Press Releases, Legislative Alerts, and Other Lobbying Materials

# LEGISLATIVE ALERT

Alert #101-12                                                    July 30, 1990

## HOUSE APPROVES FY 1991 SPENDING: SENATE ACTION EXPECTED SHORTLY

**Action Needed:** Contact Senators on the Labor, Health and Human Services Subcommittee to urge them to appropriate sufficient funds for mental health programs.

**Back-Ground:** Mental health programs have not fared well in the appropriations process so far. The House has approved its version of the FY 1991 spending bill, making inadequate increases in mental health research, deferring action on several programs because the authorizing laws have not yet been enacted, and level funding, or cutting spending on several mental health services programs.

**Senate To Act:** The Senate will act on this bill in early September, and mental health advocates are anxious to improve on the House numbers at that time. It is very important that Senators hear from their constituents that the House actions are inadequate, even in a time of fiscal constraint. NIMH programs have not fared as well in the House bill as have programs for other biomedical research or many other human services programs.

**Action Needed:** Urge Senators to provide increased funding (as per NMHA recommendations in the chart on page 2), and highlight the following needs:

- ■ Increased **research** funding for all NIMH research areas including implementation of the National Research Plan for Children and Adolescents with Mental Disorders;

- ■ Increased spending on **mental health services** programs, particularly demonstration programs for children, adults with serious mental illnesses and prevention, funds for Protection and Advocacy services and state Alcohol, Drug Abuse and Mental Health block grant funding;

- ■ Additional funding for programs to aid **homeless** persons who have a mental illness.

The need for and effectiveness of these programs is well documented. Without funding increases, research advances will be slowed, and people in need will not be able to obtain the services they need.

**ACT TODAY! Write:** Write to your Senator if he is a Member of the Subcommittee (see below). If not, write to Chairman Tom Harkin or Ranking Republican Arlen Specter. The Honorable _____, United States Senate, Washington, D.C. 20510

**Subcommittee Members:** Tom Harkin (D-IA), Chair, Robert C. Byrd (D-WV), Ernest Hollings (D-SC), Quentin N. Burdick (D-ND), Daniel K. Inouye (D-HI), Dale Bumpers (D-AR), Harry Reid (D-NV), Brock Adams (D-WA), Arlen Specter (R-PA), ranking minority member, Mark Hatfield (R-OR), Ted Stevens (R-AK), Warren Rudman (R-NH), James McClure (R-ID), Thad Cochran (R-MS) and Phil Gramm (R-TX).

Department of Public Policy, National Mental Health Association, 1021 Prince Street, Alexandria, Virginia 22314-2971
(703) 684-7722    FAX (703) 684-5968

|  | Actual Spending | President's Request | House Recommd. | NMHA Recc. |
|---|---|---|---|---|
| **NIMH** | | | | |
| Mental Health Research | $429.6 | $456.1 | $472.6 | $627.8 |
| Research Training | $ 24.2 | $ 25.8 | deferred* | $ 47.6 |
| Clinical Training | $ 13.5 | $ 5.0 | $ 13.5 | $ 29.0 |
| CSP & CASSP Service Demos. | $ 28.3 | $ 26.8 | deferred* | $ 41.0 |
| (Of which: Prevention) | ( 4.0) | ( 4.0) | deferred* | $ 5.0 |
| Homeless Services Demos. | $ 6.0 | $ 6.0 | $ 6.0 | $ 6.0 |
| Protection and Advocacy | $ 14.0 | $ 8.0 | $ 14.0 | $ 24.0 |
| State Planning Grants | $ 0 | $ 0 | $ 0 | $ 10.0 |
| **Al.,Drug & MH Admin.** | | | | |
| Homeless State Grants | $ 27.8 | $ 33.7 | $ 29.0 | $100.0 |
| ADM Block Grant: MH portion | $237.6 | $237.6 | $237.6 | $237.6 |

* pending reauthorization

## ADA ENACTED: NEED TO THANK ALL LEADERS AND SUPPORTERS

On July 26, President Bush signed into law legislation which will dramatically improve the rights of people with disabilities, including those with mental disabilities. The Americans with Disabilities Act prohibits discrimination against people with disabilities in employment in the private sector, public accommodations, private and public transportation, and telecommunications. Approximately 43 million Americans with physical and mental disabilities will be protected under the ADA, which passed the House by a vote of 377-28 and the Senate by 91-6.

The votes for final passage ended a several year struggle by leading Congressional supporters Senators Tom Harkin (D-IA), Edward Kennedy (D-MA) and Orrin Hatch, (R-UT) and Congressman Steny Hoyer (D-MD). ADA was endorsed by all major disability organizations and supported by a massive grass roots campaign, including MHAs across the country.

A summary of the bill's impact on persons with mental disabilities is being prepared and will be available from NMHA shortly.

Listed below are Members who did not vote for ADA. If your Senators and Representative are not on these lists, please write and thank them for their support of this landmark legislation.

House: Voting against: Stump (R-AZ), Herger (R-CA), Shumway (R-CA), Lewis (R-CA), Dannemeyer (R-CA), Packard (R-CA), Crane (R-IL), Hastert (R-IL), Burton (R-IN), Lightfoot (R-IA), Holloway (R-LA), Parker (D-MS), Hancock (R-MO), Marlenee (R-MT), McEwen (R-OH), Miller (R-OH), Edwards (R-OK), Shuster (R-PA), Cooper (D-TN), Archer (R-TX), Armey (R-TX), Stenholm (D-TX), Chapman (D-TX), DeLay (R-TX), Armey (R-TX), Nielson (R-UT), Bateman (R-VA), Olin (D-VA). Not voting Robinson (R-AR), Martinez (D-CA), Morrison (D-CT), Nelson (D-FL), Hatcher (D-GA), Jones (D-GA), Jenkins (D-GA), Huckaby (D-LA), Pursell (R-MI), Traxler (D-MI), Schuette (R-MI), Crockett (D-MI), Ford (D-MI), Sikorski (D-MN), Torricelli (D-NJ), Guarini (D-NJ), Flake (D-NY), Scheuer (D-NY), Schumer (D-NY), Lukens (R-OH), Gray (D-PA), McDade (R-PA), Goodling (R-PA), Ford (D-TN), Hall (D-TX), Smith (R-TX), Chandler (R-WA).

Senate: Voting against: Bond (R-MO), Garn (R-UT), Helms (R-NC), Humphrey (R-NH), Symms (R-ID) and Wallop (R-WY). Not present: McClure (R-IN), Rockefeller (D-WV) and Simpson (R-WY).

**PUBLIC**

**ISSUES**

Alert #7/90
October 11, 1990
Divisions: ALL
Deadline: October 12,

## ! ! !  URGENT  ! ! !

The Senate and the House of Representatives will be voting on a budget resolution within the next few days that includes many issues of concern to the American Cancer Society. Among these are: 1) a floor on the deductibility of charitable contributions; 2) increasing the federal cigarette excise tax; 3) funding of the "Breast and Cervical Cancer Mortality Prevention Act;" and 4) Medicare reimbursement for screening mammography.

The debates are occurring on the floors of both houses now, and votes could come at any time. It is critical that Members of your Congressional Delegation be contacted **immediately** to relay the following messages.

### CHARITABLE DEDUCTIONS

The resolution that was passed by the House Ways and Means Committee would limit the deductibility of charitable contributions. **MESSAGE: "PLEASE DO NOT LIMIT THE TAX DEDUCTION FOR INDIVIDUALS WHO MAKE CHARITABLE CONTRIBUTIONS."**

### FEDERAL CIGARETTE EXCISE TAX

The resolution currently contains an increase in the federal cigarette excise tax of 4 cents for FY 1991, with an additional 4 cent increase in FY 1993. ACS has been advocating a 16 cent increase. **MESSAGE: "PLEASE INCREASE THE FEDERAL CIGARETTE EXCISE TAX BY 16 CENTS."**

### FUNDING FOR BREAST AND CERVICAL CANCER GRANT PROGRAM

Although the "Breast and Cervical Cancer Mortality Prevention Act" was signed by the President in August, there is a possibility that funding for the program will not be included in the budget. **MESSAGE: "PLEASE INCLUDE FULL FUNDING FOR THE 'BREAST AND CERVICAL CANCER MORTALITY PREVENTION ACT' AT $50 MILLION FOR FY 1991."**

### MEDICARE COVERAGE FOR SCREENING MAMMOGRAPHY

None of the Medicare mammography bills have been included in the Medicare packages. **MESSAGE: "PLEASE EXPAND MEDICARE TO INCLUDE COVERAGE FOR SCREENING MAMMOGRAPHY."**

ERTALERTALERTALERTALE

**YMCA of the USA**
Washington Office
1701 K Street N.W., Suite 903
Washington, D.C. 20006
202-835-9043

**Harold Davis**
Chairman, National Board

**David R. Mercer**
National Executive Director

October 9, 1990

## The Business Coalition For Fair Competition's Threatened United Way Boycott -- A YMCA Response

In a recent memo, the Business Coalition for Fair Competition (BCFC) urged its members to boycott their local United Ways until they are assured that no United Way funds will go to YMCAs or other tax-exempt agencies that compete with for-profit businesses. The YMCA of the USA strongly urges United Ways to reject the BCFC's threat to YMCAs and other nonprofit human care agencies.

**The existence of for-profit providers of human care services does not eliminate the need for nonprofits.** While the BCFC memo singles out YMCA health and fitness programs, the logic of the BCFC attack extends to any nonprofit agency offering services also provided by for-profits. This includes hospitals, nursing homes, child care centers, family counseling agencies, sheltered workshops, substance abuse treatment centers, and home health care agencies. Nonprofits pioneered each of these services. However, the BCFC apparently believes that as soon as for-profit firms enter a field, the need for nonprofits disappears. This simplistic (and self-serving) position ignores the fact that YMCAs and other nonprofits provide important community benefits that for-profit providers of similar services never will.

**Important differences between nonprofit and for-profit providers of human care services justify their different tax treatment:**

* **For-profits serve only persons they can serve at a profit; nonprofits accept a responsibility to serve the whole community, including those who cannot pay the market rate.** For example, YMCAs routinely provide financial assistance to needy adults and families who want to participate in YMCA health and fitness programs. YMCAs also provide specialized fitness programs for seniors, handicapped persons, and others with special needs. In all of these ways, YMCAs and other nonprofits bring diverse groups together and, in the process, help build stronger communities.

**YMCA Mission:**
To put Christian principles into practice through programs that build healthy body, mind, and spirit for all.

* **For-profits entered the human care field to make a profit; nonprofits provide human care services to meet human needs.** These different motives translate into very different operational behavior. For example, YMCAs have a hundred year track record of providing reliable, quality community fitness programs. By contrast, nearly 30 states have enacted "health spa" laws to protect the public against widespread consumer abuse in the commercial health club industry. Similarly, YMCAs have rigorous program design and staff training standards to insure high quality, medically-based programs.

* **Nonprofits provide continuity of service in good times and bad.** While for-profits have recently entered many human care fields, they can exit just as quickly when profits wane, as they have in home health care and in certain areas of hospital care. Because YMCAs and other human care nonprofits belong to their communities, they respond to long-term community needs -- not short-term profits.

* **Nonprofits mobilize community resources to meet community needs.** While for-profits depend solely on earned-income, nonprofit human care providers mobilize contributed support -- both money and volunteer services -- to meet needs that would otherwise go unmet. Thus, one of the clearest differences between YMCA adult fitness programs and commercial health clubs is that while for-profits ask for nothing beyond payment for services rendered, YMCAs challenge participants to support the overall community service mission of the YMCA through gifts of time and money.

**YMCA adult fitness programs are exempt from federal tax and are also tax-exempt in every state.** In the early 1980's the IRS conducted an intensive review of YMCA adult fitness programs. This review resulted in the current IRS "community access" rule under which a YMCA must demonstrate that its adult fitness programs serve all income levels in the community. To date, no YMCA has failed this test. YMCA adult fitness programs are also routinely exempted from tax in each of the 50 states. While for-profit health clubs have committed substantial resources to challenging YMCA tax-exemption, only two of the more than 2,000 YMCA facilities nationwide have been placed on the local tax rolls, and YMCAs are working to reverse both of these results.

## INDEPENDENT SECTOR

### THE CHARITABLE DEDUCTION FOR NONITEMIZERS
### SHOULD BE ENACTED BY CONGRESS

INDEPENDENT SECTOR supports legislation which was introduced in the House and Senate on May 9, 1990, to extend the charitable tax deduction to the 72 million nonitemizing taxpayers who presently can't deduct their contributions but clearly deserve to do so. Sponsors of the House measure, HR 4761, are Representatives Byron Dorgan (D-ND) and Rod Chandler (R-WA). Sponsors of the Senate legislation, S2601, are Senators Daniel K. Inouye (D-HI) and Robert W. Kasten (R-WI).

Congress enacted a charitable deduction for nonitemizers in 1981, which included a provision that would permit the legislation to expire at the end of 1986. The House voted in 1985 to make the legislation permanent, but the Senate defeated a similar provision by 51 to 44. The legislation was dropped in the House/Senate Tax Reform Conference and, therefore, expired at the end of 1986.

INDEPENDENT SECTOR supports reenactment of the charitable deduction for nonitemizers for a number of reasons, including:

o    Low and modest income Americans are the nation's most generous contributors. They give, as a percentage of income, 30% more to charity than the average American. Most of these modest income contributors are nonitemizers and, therefore, cannot deduct their contributions to charity.

o    The majority of nonitemizers are lower and middle income taxpayers. 91% of all nonitemizers have incomes under $30,000 a year. 97% have incomes under $40,000 a year. From the foregoing it is clear that the nonitemizer deduction would benefit greatly those modest income Americans who give so generously to a broad array of human services.

o    Nonitemizers support services such as the Red Cross, the American Cancer Society and the United Way. They give to churches and synagogues, environmental organizations, schools, colleges, and hospitals, food programs for the homeless and the Boy Scouts and Girl

A NATIONAL FORUM TO ENCOURAGE GIVING, VOLUNTEERING AND NOT • FOR • PROFIT INITIATIVE
1828 L Street, N.W. • Washington, D.C. 20036 • (202) 223-8100
SUCCESSOR TO THE COALITION OF NATIONAL VOLUNTARY ORGANIZATIONS AND THE NATIONAL COUNCIL ON PHILANTHROPY

programs for the homeless and the Boy Scouts and Girl
Scouts. They give to advocacy groups, health research,
the arts, international development and the myriad of
activities in the public interest that enrich our
society and protect its people.

o    Nonitemizers are sensitive to tax considerations.
     Charitable contributions by nonitemizers increased by
     40% or $4 billion from 1985 to 1986, according to
     Internal Revenue Service data. Nonitemizers were
     permitted to deduct only 50% of their charitable
     contributions in 1985, and they gave $9.5 billion that
     year. In 1986, they could deduct a full 100% and,
     according to the IRS, they gave $13.4 billion - an
     increase of 40%.

o    70% of respondents to a 1988 Gallup survey believed
     that people should be able to take a charitable tax
     deduction whether or not they itemized their deductions
     on their income tax returns.

o    Federal funding of human services has been cut
     drastically over the past eight years. Federal funding
     of those services have been reduced by a total of $120
     billion*, compared to what would have been spent had
     1980 federal spending levels been maintained. This, in
     turn, reduced federal support to private, nonprofit
     organizations by an estimated cumulative total of $33
     billion* over the same period. These federal budget
     cuts have increased greatly pressure on nonprofit
     organizations to seek additional sources of contributed
     income, such as the charitable deduction for
     nonitemizers.

o    Some have argued that the standard tax deduction takes
     into account any charitable deductions made by
     nonitemizers. Therefore, they contend, nonitemizers
     should not be permitted a deduction for their gifts,
     because it would, in effect, amount to a "double
     deduction." This legislation addresses any concern
     about double benefits by limiting a nonitemizer's
     deduction to that amount exceeding $100 of their
     charitable contributions. The $100 floor will help
     reduce IRS compliance concerns by reducing the number
     of potential returns for filing.

*    These figures are exclusive of spending for Medicare and
     Medicaid.

2

National
Mental Health
Association
™

**Facts**

## CHILDHOOD MENTAL DISORDERS:
## RESEARCH & SERVICES LAG ADULT FIELD

*America neglects her children who suffer from mental and emotional disorders. The Committee for Economic Development concludes that the optimal and healthy development of children is critical to U.S. productivity at home and in the world market.*

■ **7.5 million, and upwards to 14 million, children and adolescents suffer from a mental or emotional disorder.**

> NEVERTHELESS
> ■    Less than one-fifth now receive appropriate treatment, and many of those treated -- even by the best clinicians -- fail to recover because their disorders are not adequately understood.
>
> ■    Less than 20 percent of children with severe emotional disturbance eligible for special education services under the Education of All Handicapped Children Act receive such education, while 80 percent of other eligible handicapped children receive services.

■ **Dramatic advances have occurred in child and adolescent mental health research during the past two decades, which promises the hope of overcoming many puzzling disorders. Furthermore, research on childhood mental disorders is likely to clarify the cause and risk factors for many adult disorders.**

> NEVERTHELESS
> ■    The field lacks the critical mass of researchers and infusion of fresh talent, resources, and equipment needed to realize its potential.
>
> ■    Fewer than 20 child psychiatrists in the U.S. are full-time researchers, and other disciplines contribute less than their expected share of researchers, especially young researchers.
>
> ■    Less than one-half of 1¢ is spent on research in childhood mental disorders for every dollar spent in treatment. In FY 1989 only $70 million was spent by the National Institute of Mental Health to support research on childhood mental disorders, which cost the Nation more than $1.5 billion in treatment costs.

■ **Community and family-based systems of care are being emphasized by the public mental health sector in the treatment of childhood mental disorders.**

> NEVERTHELESS
> ■    Many States continue to allocate two-thirds or more of their children's mental health budget to residential or hospital treatment.

1021 Prince Street • Alexandria, Virginia 22314-2971 • (703) 684-7722 • FAX (703) 684-5968

- The Invisible Children Project of the National Mental Health Association reports about 5,000 children are placed out of their own state each year in residential treatment facilities.

- There was a 450 percent increase in placements of youth in private psychiatric facilities in the 1980s, and children with severe emotional problems have a three-time greater chance of being placed in residential care programs than mentally retarded or learning disabled students.

- Most children with mental disorders are not seen by mental health specialists, but by primary care providers, school personnel, and juvenile and social welfare staff.

Sources: National Mental Health Association (1989), *Final Report and Recommendations of the Invisible Children Project.* Office of Technology Assessment (1986), *Children's Mental Health: Problems and Services-A Background Paper.* Institute of Medicine (1989), *Research on Children & Adolescents with Mental, Behavioral & Developmental Disorders.* Committee for Economic Development (1987), *Children in Need: Investment Strategies for the Educationally Disadvantaged.*

February 1990

**INDEPENDENT
SECTOR**

August 31, 1990

MEDIA ADVISORY

NATIONAL NONPROFIT ORGANIZATIONS SPONSOR PRESS CONFERENCE ON
IMMINENT DANGER TO TAX DEDUCTIONS FOR CHARITABLE CONTRIBUTIONS

> Contact:
> John Thomas
> Bob Smucker
> INDEPENDENT SECTOR
> 202) 223-8100
>
> Bebe Bahnsen
> Alison Meares
> Bahnsen Communications
> (202) 387-6556

Administration and congressional budget summiteers have said they
will consider all potential sources of revenue in their search to
reduce the federal deficit, including limitations on remaining
tax deductions. This threat to the tax deduction for charitable
contributions is a major concern of national nonprofit
organizations representing religious, educational, social service
and cultural institutions and agencies around the country.

INDEPENDENT SECTOR, a coalition of 700 corporate, foundation and
voluntary organizations whose mission is to encourage giving,
volunteering and not-for-profit initiatives, will sponsor a **press
conference at 10:00 a.m. Wednesday, September 5 in the East Room,
National Press Club.** National leaders of major nonprofit
organizations will explain the devastating impact that abolishing
or limiting the tax deductibility of charitable gifts would have
on their organizations and the people they serve.

Speakers will include:

   **Brian O'Connell, President Independent Sector
   Father Thomas J. Harvey, Executive Director, Catholic
      Charities USA
   Robert H. Atwell, President, American Council on Education.
   Robert P. Dugan, Jr., Director, Office of Public Affairs,
      National Association of Evangelicals**

A NATIONAL FORUM TO ENCOURAGE GIVING, VOLUNTEERING AND NOT · FOR · PROFIT INITIATIVE
1828 L Street, N.W. · Washington, D.C. 20036 · (202) 223-8100
SUCCESSOR TO THE COALITION OF NATIONAL VOLUNTARY ORGANIZATIONS AND THE NATIONAL COUNCIL ON PHILANTHROPY

## INDEPENDENT
## SECTOR

# NEWS RELEASE

**FOR IMMEDIATE RELEASE**               Contact:   Bob Smucker
                                                    John Thomas
                                                    202/223-8100

### CHARITABLE DEDUCTION FOR ITEMIZERS THREATENED

**Budget Negotiators Consider Additional Limitations
on Individual Itemized Tax Deductions**

Washington, D.C., August 6, 1990 -- As one means of
raising revenue to deal with the federal deficit, budget
negotiators from Congress and the Administration are
considering additional limitations on charitable deductions.
This would be the fourth major undercutting of the very side
of our society to which government is trying to transfer so
much responsibility for public service.

"For an Administration and Congress committed
philosophically and practically to expansion of local
volunteer organizations and services, it is a contradiction
to look to the voluntary sector for additional funds and
increased services.  The regulators can't have it both
ways," said Brian O'Connell, President of INDEPENDENT SECTOR
(**IS**), a Washington-based coalition of over 700 foundations,
corporations and not-for-profit groups.

"Cutting back on the deductibility of charitable
contributions not only would exacerbate the difficult
problems charities presently face in meeting a wide range of
human needs, but is not consistent with long-standing public
policy which has always sought ways to foster private
initiative for the public good.

"Deductions for charitable contributions are not like
any of the other tax deductions.  The contributions do not
represent any advantage to the giver, and they still are a
subtraction from what one could spend on other things.
These are not dollars consumed or saved.  They are
voluntarily contributed for public purposes.

A NATIONAL FORUM TO ENCOURAGE GIVING, VOLUNTEERING AND NOT · FOR · PROFIT INITIATIVE
1828 L Street, N.W. · Washington, D.C. 20036 ● (202) 223-8100
SUCCESSOR TO THE COALITION OF NATIONAL VOLUNTARY ORGANIZATIONS AND THE NATIONAL COUNCIL ON PHILANTHROPY.

"In addition, capping or otherwise limiting how much people can deduct doesn't just impact potential contributors. It undermines all of the causes and people served by the organizations for which gifts will be reduced."

Congress, in 1986, ended charitable tax deductions for 72 million Americans who do not itemize their tax deductions. At the same time, Congress made gifts of appreciated property subject of the Alternative Minimum Tax. These reductions in the tax incentives for charitable contributions are in addition to cuts in federal spending for human services which have totaled $120 billion from 1982 to 1989, exclusive of Medicare and Medicaid. Of that $120 billion, a total of $32 billion was cut from services provided by nonprofits.

Additional reasons IS is backing the charitable deduction for itemizers include:

- Individual giving is the lifeblood of the independent sector, and tax incentives are critical to how much individuals give. For every $1.00 the government does not garner due to the charitable deduction, the charitable sector gains between $1.09 and $1.29. It is a kind of voluntary tax. It permits the exercise of a full range of individual choices by the taxpayer about what public purposes to support.

- It is conceivable that, at first, the amount the charitable deduction would be decreased in value would be modest, but it would start the deduction down the same slope as the tax deduction for medical expenses. Over the years, Congress reduced the medical deduction to the point that now taxpayers can deduct only one-half of what they could 20 years ago. There is every reason to believe that charitable deductions would go the same way.

- The 1986 Tax Reform Act had an especially adverse impact on contributions by upper income people. Those with incomes of $1 million or more gave an average of $200,000 in 1986, and less than half that amount, $93,000 in 1987, the first year after tax reform. For the seven years prior to tax reform, giving had never been less than $138,000 for that income group, so it is very clear that giving from that group was affected significantly by the 1986 Tax Reform Act.

(more)

- A broad array of services benefit from the increased
  giving for charitable causes, including protection for
  the environment, health research, food programs for the
  homeless, schools and colleges, refugee crisis
  counseling, youth services, civil rights, hospitals,
  community and international development, the arts,
  housing for senior citizens, and the myriad of activities
  in the public interest that enrich our society and
  protect its people.

INDEPENDENT SECTOR and its 700 member organizations are
urging Congress and the Administration to drop the proposal
to cut the charitable tax deduction.

# # #

INDEPENDENT SECTOR is a nonprofit coalition of 700
corporate, foundation and voluntary organization members
with national interest and impact in philanthropy and
voluntary action. The organization's mission is to create a
national forum capable of encouraging the giving,
volunteering and not-for-profit initiative that helps all of
us better serve people, communities and causes.

# Resource E

## IRS
## Form 5768

| Form **5768** | Election/Revocation of Election by an Eligible Section 501(c)(3) Organization To Make Expenditures To Influence Legislation | |
|---|---|---|
| (Rev. January 1990) Department of the Treasury Internal Revenue Service | (Under Section 501(h) of the Internal Revenue Code) | For IRS Use Only ▶ |

| Name of organization | Employer identification number |
|---|---|

Address (number and street)

City or town, state, and ZIP code

**1  Election.**—As an eligible organization we hereby elect to have the provisions of section 501(h) of the Code, relating to expenditures to influence legislation, apply to our tax year ending _____ and all subsequent tax years until revoked.

(Month, day, and year)

**Note:** *This election must be signed and postmarked within the first taxable year to which it applies.*

**2  Revocation.**—As an eligible organization we hereby revoke our election to have the provisions of section 501(h) of the Code, relating to expenditures to influence legislation, apply to our tax year ending _____

(Month, day, and year)

**Note:** *This revocation must be signed and postmarked before the first day of the tax year to which it applies.*

Under penalties of perjury, I declare that I am authorized to make this (check applicable box) ▶ ☐ election/ ☐ revocation on behalf of the above named organization.

| (Signature of officer or trustee) | (Title) | (Date) |
|---|---|---|

## Instructions

*(References are to the Internal Revenue Code.)*

Section 501(c)(3) provides that an organization exempt under that section will lose its tax-exempt status and its qualification to receive deductible charitable contributions if a substantial part of its activities are carried on to influence legislation. Section 501(h), however, permits certain eligible 501(c)(3) organizations to elect to make limited expenditures to influence legislation. An organization making the election will, however, be subject to an excise tax under section 4911 if it spends more than the amounts permitted by that section. Furthermore, the organization may lose its exempt status if its lobbying expenditures exceed the permitted amounts by more than 50% over a 4-year period. For any tax year in which an election under section 501(h) is in effect, an electing organization must report the actual and permitted amounts of its lobbying expenditures and grass roots expenditures (as defined in section 4911(c)) on its annual return required under section 6033. See Schedule A (Form 990). Each electing member of an affiliated group must report these amounts for both itself and the affiliated group as a whole.

To make or revoke the election, enter the ending date of the tax year to which the election or revocation applies in item 1 or 2, as applicable, and sign and date the form in the spaces provided.

**Eligible Organizations.**—A section 501(c)(3) organization is permitted to make the election if it is not a disqualified organization (see below) and is described in:

*(a)* section 170(b)(1)(A)(ii) (relating to educational institutions),

*(b)* section 170(b)(1)(A)(iii) (relating to hospitals and medical research organizations),

*(c)* section 170(b)(1)(A)(iv) (relating to organizations supporting government schools),

*(d)* section 170(b)(1)(A)(vi) (relating to organizations publicly supported by charitable contributions),

*(e)* section 509(a)(2) (relating to organizations publicly supported by admissions, sales, etc.), or

*(f)* section 509(a)(3) (relating to organizations supporting certain types of public charities other than those section 509(a)(3) organizations that support section 501(c)(4), (5), or (6) organizations).

**Disqualified Organizations.**—The following types of organizations are not permitted to make the election:

*(a)* section 170(b)(1)(A)(i) organizations (relating to churches),

*(b)* an integrated auxiliary of a church or of a convention or association of churches, or

*(c)* a member of an affiliated group of organizations if one or more members of such group is described in (a) or (b) of this paragraph.

**Affiliated Organizations.**—Organizations are members of an affiliated group of organizations only if: (1) the governing instrument of one such organization requires it to be bound by the decisions of the other organization on legislative issues, or (2) the governing board of one such organization includes persons who (i) are specifically designated representatives of another such organization or are members of the governing board, officers, or paid executive staff members of such other organization, and (ii) by aggregating their votes have sufficient voting power to cause or prevent action on legislative issues by the first such organization.

For more details, see section 4911 and section 501(h).

**Note:** *A private foundation (including a private operating foundation) is not an eligible organization.*

**Where To File.**—Mail Form 5768 to the applicable **Internal Revenue Service Center** listed below.

| If the principal office of the organization is located in: | Use this address: |
|---|---|
| Alabama, Arkansas, Florida, Georgia, Louisiana, Mississippi, North Carolina, South Carolina, Tennessee | Atlanta, GA 39901 |
| Arizona, Colorado, Kansas, New Mexico, Oklahoma, Texas, Utah, Wyoming | Austin, TX 73301 |
| Indiana, Kentucky, Michigan, Ohio, West Virginia | Cincinnati, OH 45999 |
| Alaska, California, Hawaii, Idaho, Nevada, Oregon, Washington | Fresno, CA 93888 |
| Connecticut, Delaware, Maine, Massachusetts, New Hampshire, New Jersey, New York, Pennsylvania (ZIP codes beginning with 169–171 and 173–196 only), Rhode Island, Vermont | Holtsville, NY 00501 |
| Illinois, Iowa, Minnesota, Missouri, Montana, Nebraska, North Dakota, South Dakota, Wisconsin | Kansas City, MO 64999 |
| District of Columbia, Maryland, Pennsylvania (ZIP codes beginning with 150–168 and 172 only), Virginia, any U.S. possession, any foreign country | Philadelphia, PA 19255 |

Form **5768** (Rev 1-90)

# Resource F

# Organizations and Information

## Organizations

The Advocacy Institute, 1730 Rhode Island Ave., N.W., Suite 600, Washington, DC 20036.

Common Cause, 2030 M St., N.W., Washington, DC 20036.

INDEPENDENT SECTOR, 1828 L St., N.W., Washington, DC 20003. Tel.: (202) 223-8100.

## Information

To obtain IRS Form 5768:

| Location of Principal Office | Where to Write |
| --- | --- |
| Alabama, Arkansas, Florida, Georgia, Louisiana, Mississippi, North Carolina, South Carolina, Tennessee | IRS Atlanta, GA 39901 |
| Arizona, Colorado, Kansas, New Mexico, Oklahoma, Texas, Utah, Wyoming | IRS Austin, TX 73301 |
| Indiana, Kentucky, Michigan, Ohio, West Virginia | IRS Cincinnati, OH 45999 |

| | |
|---|---|
| Alaska, California, Hawaii, Idaho, Nevada, Oregon, Washington | IRS Fresno, CA 93888 |
| Connecticut, Delaware, Maine, Massachusetts, New Hampshire, New Jersey, New York, Pennsylvania (ZIP codes beginning with 169–272 and 173–196 only), Rhode Island, Vermont | IRS Holtsville, NY 00501 |
| Illinois, Iowa, Minnesota, Missouri, Montana, Nebraska, North Dakota, South Dakota, Wisconsin | IRS Kansas City, MO 64999 |
| District of Columbia, Maryland, Pennsylvania (ZIP codes beginning with 150–168 and 172 only), Virginia, any U.S. possession, any foreign country | IRS Philadelphia, PA 19255 |

For nonprofit organizations that want to register to lobby, contact the following for information:

Secretary of the U.S. Senate, S-208 Capitol Building, Washington, DC 20510. Tel.: (202) 224-3622.

Clerk of the U.S. House of Representatives, H-105 Capitol Building, Washington, DC 20515. Tel.: (202) 225-7000.

# REFERENCES

American Arts Alliance. *Handbook on Advocacy*. Washington, D.C.: American Arts Alliance, n.d.

American Council for the Arts. *ACA Update*. New York: American Council for the Arts, 1983.

American Heart Association. *Heart and Government: A Guide to Lobbying*. Washington, D.C.: American Heart Association, 1984.

American Lung Association. *Legislative Network Volunteer Manual*. New York: American Lung Association, 1985.

Association of Junior Leagues. *By the People*. New York: Association of Junior Leagues, 1986.

Barry, J. M. *Lobbying for the People*. Princeton, N.J.: Princeton University Press, 1977.

Burson-Marsteller. *Special Washington Report: Communications and Congress: A Study of the Exposure of Federal Legislative Offices to Various Information Vehicles*. Washington, D.C.: Burson-Marsteller, 1981.

Children's Defense Fund. *Lobbying and Political Activity for Nonprofits: What You Can (and Can't) Do Under Federal Law*. Washington, D.C.: Children's Defense Fund, 1983.

Common Cause. *Action Manual*. Washington, D.C.: Common Cause, n.d.

Common Cause. *Citizens Action Guide*. Washington, D.C.: Common Cause, n.d.

Common Cause. *Tips on Effective Lobbying.* Washington, D.C.: Common Cause, n.d.

Duncan, P. *Politics in America, 1990: The 101st Congress.* Washington, D.C.: Congressional Quarterly Press, 1989.

Gardner, J. W. *In Common Cause.* New York: Norton, 1972.

Goodwill Industries of America, Inc. *A Working Partnership—You and Your Government.* Washington, D.C.: Goodwill Industries of America, Inc., 1981.

Grupenhoff, J. T., and Murphy, J. J. *Nonprofits' Handbook on Lobbying.* Washington, D.C.: Taft Corporation, 1977.

Halperin, S. *A Guide for the Powerless—and Those Who Don't Know Their Own Power.* Washington, D.C.: Institution for Educational Leadership, 1981.

Hubbard, R. L. *Lobbying by Public Charities.* Washington, D.C.: National Center for Voluntary Action/Council for Public Interest Law, 1977.

INDEPENDENT SECTOR. *Permissible Activities of 501(c) Organizations During a Political Campaign.* (Rev. ed.) Washington, D.C.: INDEPENDENT SECTOR, 1987.

INDEPENDENT SECTOR. *Lobby? You?* Washington, D.C.: INDEPENDENT SECTOR, n.d.

Internal Revenue Service. *Revenue Ruling E:O:1-1.* Washington, D.C.: Internal Revenue Service, 1977.

League of Women Voters of the United States. *Making an Issue of It: The Campaign Handbook.* Washington, D.C.: League of Women Voters of the United States, 1976.

League of Women Voters of the United States. *Tell It to Washington.* Washington, D.C.: League of Women Voters of the United States, 1979.

Lustberg, A. *Testifying with Impact.* Washington, D.C.: U.S. Chamber of Commerce, 1982.

Marlowe, H. "Unresolved Issues Confronting Private Foundations Making Grants to Public Charities Which May Use Funds for Lobbying." *Washington Foundation Journal,* Oct. 17, 1978.

Marlowe, H. *How to Talk So Congress Listens: A Manual for Nonprofits.* Washington, D.C.: Washington Nonprofit Services, 1979.

National Family Planning and Reproductive Health Association.

*Grassroots Lobbying.* Washington, D.C.: National Family Planning and Reproductive Health Association, 1981.

National Mental Health Association. *A Layman's Guide to Lobbying Without Losing Your Tax-Exempt Status.* Alexandria, Va.: National Mental Health Association, 1989.

National Society for Children and Adults with Autism. *NSAC Action.* Washington, D.C.: National Society for Children and Adults with Autism, 1985.

O'Connell, B. *Effective Leadership in Voluntary Organizations.* New York: Walker & Co., 1976.

O'Connell, B. *The Board Members Book.* New York: Foundation Center, 1985.

Ornstein, N. J., and Elder, S. *Interest Groups, Lobbying and Policy Making.* Washington, D.C.: Congressional Quarterly Press, 1978.

*Regan* v. *Taxation With Representation of Washington,* 461 U.S. 540, 545 n. 6 (1983).

Talisman, M. E. *The Legislative Process.* Washington, D.C.: Council of Jewish Federations, 1977.

Webster, G. D., and Krebs, F. J. *Association and Lobbying Regulation.* Washington, D.C.: U.S. Chamber of Commerce, 1985.

Willett, E. F., Jr. *How Our Laws Are Made.* Washington, D.C.: U.S. Government Printing Office, 1990.

# INDEX